Journal of the Fantastic in the Arts
Volume 33/ Number 1

JFA

Journal of the Fantastic in the Arts
Volume 33/ Number 1

FAVIAN PRESS

A FAVIAN PRESS PAPERBACK

© Copyright 2023
JFA

The right of JFA to be identified as author of this work has been asserted in accordance with the Copyright, Designs and Patents Act 1988

All Rights Reserved

No reproduction, copy or transmission of the publication may be made without written permission. No paragraph of this publication may be reproduced, copied or transmitted save with the written permission of the publisher, or in accordance with the provisions of the Copyright Act 1956 (as amended).

Any person who does any unauthorised act in relation to this publication may be liable to criminal prosecution and civil claims for damages.

ISBN 978 1 78695 831 0

This edition published 2023
by Favian Press
an imprint of
Fiction4All
www.fiction4all.com

Journal of the Fantastic in the Arts
Volume 33/ Number 1
Whole Number 113
Supported by the
International Association for the Fantastic in the Arts.
Printed in the United States of America.

Managing Editor-in-Chief	Jude Wright
Reviews Editor-in-Chief	Mailyn Abreu Toribio
Acquisitions Editor-in-Chief	Novella Brooks de Vita
Production Editor-in-Chief	Cat Ashton
Senior Submissions and Reviews Editor	Farah Mendlesohn

GENERAL INQUIRIES
Inquiries and other editorial correspondence should be directed to jfa.editor@fantastic-arts.org.

SUBMISSIONS
Like the International Conference on the Fantastic in the Arts, *JFA* welcomes papers on all aspects of the fantastic in world literatures and media, as well as interdisciplinary approaches including African/Diaspora Studies, anthropology, area studies, critical game studies, disability studies, future studies, gender studies, history, Indigenous studies, music, philosophy, political science, postcolonial studies, psychology, queer studies, religious studies, science and technology studies, and sociology. All papers are made available in English and fully refereed. The journal is indexed in the MLA Bibliography.

Submissions should contain a more in-depth discussion than a conference-length paper and demonstrate a grasp of current scholarship on the subject. The length of articles generally varies from 3,500-9,000 words and ranges from 15-35 pages.

All submissions are peer-reviewed in accordance with our peer review statement and the BIPOC Anti-Racist Statement on Scholarly Reviewing Practices. If submissions are flagged at any point of the review process for the risk of promulgating potentially misrepresentative, stereotypical, ableist, or racist views, contributors will be asked to address these problems before the review process can continue.

Since the refereeing process is anonymous, the author's name should not appear anywhere on the text file itself, including the notes. No title page is needed. However, an abstract of 100-150 words should be included with each submission.

Please ensure that all citations and the Works Cited entries are in MLA style, 9th Edition. Please enter end notes manually.

Contributors are responsible for acquiring all permissions to quote and/or use illustrations that accompany their article, and for paying (or arranging to have their institutions pay) all usage fees, including copyright.

Scholarly articles should be directed to the JFA's Acquisitions Editor-in-Chief, Novella Brooks de Vita at jfa.acquisitions@fantastic-arts.org.

BOOK REVIEWS
JFA also publishes reviews of scholarly works addressing the fantastic, broadly construed. Reviews of fiction are limited to reissues of speculative works with new introductions and scholarly apparatuses, and speculative works with the potential to impact scholarship in the genre. Books and other media received are advertised on the IAFA discussion list (which can be subscribed to through the IAFA homepage at www.iafa.org), and IAFA members are encouraged to suggest titles for review.

To mail book copies for review and for queries or reviews of English-language publications, please contact Reviews Editor-in-Chief Mailyn Abreu Toribio at jfa.bookreview@fantastic-arts.org.

Contents

Images of Horror: Black Childhood as a Site of Resistance in Visual Media   12
   Sara Austin

The Emotion of Dread in Cinematic Horror   46
   Matthias De Bondt

Atomic Art and the Ecological Perspectives of David Lynch   74
   Todd Tietchen

Han Song's Weirdly Sublime Anti-Modernity   112
   Ron Judy

REVIEWS

Kevin J. Wetmore Jr.'s *The Conjuring (Devil's Advocates)* 148
   Rev. by Zachary Doiron

Tison Pugh's *Harry Potter and Beyond: On J.K. Rowling's Fantasies and Other Fictions*   152
   Rev. by Anna Lüscher

Christy Williams's *Mapping Fairy-Tale Space: Pastiche and Metafiction in Borderless Tales*   158
   Rev. by Alexandra Lykissas

Kyle A. Moody and Nicholas Yanes's *Hannibal for Dinner: Essays on America's Favorite Cannibal on Television*   164
   Rev. by Kathleen Shaughnessy

Laurence Rickels's *Critique of Fantasy, Vol 1: Between a Crypt and a Datemark*, *Critique of Fantasy, Vol 2: The Contest Between B-Genres*, and *Critique of Fantasy, Vol 3: The Block of Fame*   170
   Rev. by Brian Willems

Abstracts

Sara Austin
Images of Horror: Black Childhood as a Site of Resistance in Visual Media

Child characters in Black horror interact with the monstrous as a means of resistance to racist violence. In this article, I examine how visual examples of Black horror, including the television series *Lovecraft Country* (2020), picture books *Wee Winnie Witch's Skinny* (2004) and *Precious and the Boo Hag* (2005), and the film *Us* (2019), re-center Black child subjectivity from images of the body in pain onto community belonging by challenging both the audience and subject divides between the child and adult. These examples acknowledge that threats to Black subjectivity are continuous, but the family remains, grows, and passes on art and love to the next generation. This bringing-together of adults, children, families, and neighbors carries a powerful message of belonging and value as its own Radical Aesthetic within Black horror.

Matthias De Bondt
The Emotion of Dread in Cinematic Horror

This article concerns itself with the cinematic emotion of dread. Within Horror Studies, cinematic dread has been theorized as a temporal emotion, mostly centered around the confrontation with the monstrous, after which dread evolves into other cinematic emotions of shock and/or horror. For this reason, the function of dread within the horror film experience is only recognized in relation to other emotions it should precede. However, this article argues that dread plays a crucial emotion in the affective workings of some horror films that fall under the term "dread-full" films. Through the close reading of two case studies, namely *It Comes At Night* and *The Blackcoat's Daughter*, the article reasons that dread exists as an inseparable part of the viewing experience of these films and in doing so, argues that the emotion of dread is *inherent* to the overall cinematic horror experience.

Todd Tietchen
Atomic Art and the Ecological Perspectives of David Lynch

The work of David Lynch represents an essential engagement with the Anthropocene and its aesthetic forms. This is especially evident in the case of *Twin Peaks*, which integrates influences from multiple genres and the avant-garde into a complex mythopoeic treatment of planetary ecological crisis. Episode eight of *Twin Peaks: The Return*, with its Promethean title "Gotta Light?", grounds Lynch's mythopoesis in an origin story that builds upon foundational concepts regarding the Anthropocene, including its connections to the atomic age, its grounding suppositions in androcentrism, its complicity in cosmological violence, and the value of post-nature perspectives for understanding the (perhaps inescapably) precarious present.

Ron Judy
Han Song's Weirdly Sublime Anti-Modernity

Han Song is a leading 21st-century Chinese science fiction author, but writes with great pathos about a modernity populated by monsters and perverse new social arrangements. From the aeronautical cannibalism of "The Passengers and the Creator" to the ghost labor of "Regenerated Bricks" and zombified workers of "My Fatherland Does Not Dream," Han's oeuvre repeatedly emphasizes the demented, and according to him "foreign" aspects of China's passage into the globalized modernity. In this article I argue that, in the aforementioned novellas Han projects a consistent vision of a "weird modernity" that is at times deeply ethnocentric, localist, and reminiscent of the "Old Weird" authors of the early 20th-century (e.g., H.P. Lovecraft, Robert E. Howard, Seabury Quinn, and Clark Ashton Smith). Reading his work's anti-modern pathos as a variant of weird fiction enables me to incorporate a Lacanian analysis of his racial others in terms of "enjoyment theft" borrowed from Slavoj Zizek. Han's work is thus a gallery of unspeakable "sublime objects" that represent the weird potential and threat of modernity—i.e., it expresses China's still deep-seated anxieties about "opening up" to an alien, non-Chinese "outside" world that seeks to steal, exploit, or subvert its desires.

Images of Horror: Black Childhood as a Site of Resistance in Visual Media

Sara Austin

TOPSY IS A CURSE. She and her twin, Bopsy, twirl and caper through the corners and backgrounds of their victims' vision. Their matted hair is tied with red string. Broken teeth show behind too-wide smiles as foot-long nails reach out to slice and scar, turning the living flesh of unsuspecting children into death and desiccation. They never stop the pursuit. Their touch is inevitable. In season 1, episode 8 of Misha Green's *Lovecraft Country*, "Jig-A-Bobo," Seamus Lancaster (Mac Brandt), a police captain and literal wizard in a white supremacist cult, summons Topsy (Kaelynn Gobert-Harris) and Bopsy (Bianca Brewton) to kill Diana Freeman (Jada Harris) after she runs away from her friend Emmett Till's funeral (Green "Jig-A-Bobo"). *Lovecraft Country's* use of Diana and Till act as recent examples of this essay's focus: Black horror uses visual symbols to empower children who have been subjected to the monstrosity of white violence and centers them in multigenerational narratives of community support.

Topsy originates as a racist caricature in Harriet Beecher Stowe's *Uncle Tom's Cabin* (1852) where her laziness and general disregard for herself and others act as a foil to the innocent perfection of the white child, Eva. Eva's goodness persuades Topsy to change her ways, aligning with cultural expectations for race and childhood in the 1850s. The novel describes Topsy as:

> "one of the blackest of her race; [. . .] Her woolly hair was braided in sundry little tails, which stuck out in every direction. The expression of her face was an odd mixture of shrewdness and cunning, over which was oddly drawn, like a kind of veil, an expression of the most doleful gravity and solemnity. She was dressed in a single filthy, ragged garment, made of bagging; and stood with her hands demurely folded before her. Altogether, there was something odd and goblin-like about her appearance[.]" (Stowe 202)

As Stowe's novel is transmuted into other cultural forms, such as plays and material culture, Topsy becomes a minstrel character. Jim O'Loughlin explains that as Stowe's novel migrated to the stage, the sentimental aspects of Topsy's character fell away and "as laughter replaced tears, representations of Topsy began to do quite different cultural work" (O'Loughlin 582). Topsy is unreformed and incorrigible in the staged versions of the novel, and so the violence done to her body is a source of amusement for white audiences, and of disgust and horror for Black audiences.

The depiction of Topsy in *Lovecraft Country* draws heavily on this minstrel tradition through the use of costuming, highlighting an over-large mouth with red lips that match the ribbons in her matted hair. These hints of red stand out against her skin and drab sackcloth dress, emphasizing the visual symbols of minstrelsy, and its associated violence against Black bodies as a source of horror. As Till's death in the series draws on the audience's knowledge of real-world physical violence and intergenerational trauma, Diana's attempts to flee Topsy and Bopsy illustrate the burden these characters, and other racist tropes like them, place onto Black children.

Black horror layers visual symbols in ways that allow for a slippage in visual media theory. Reading picture books through a film theory lens, and films through the lens of picture book theory, highlights the critical role of the Black child as a valued and agentic community member in Black horror. Though Black horror film has been discussed at length by various scholars, I read Black horror films, television, and picture books alongside one another to develop a more comprehensive theoretical framework for how visual layering works to both empower Black children within Black horror and refocus the genre from narratives of Black bodies in pain into narratives of community rebuilding and belonging. Through depictions of intergenerational families, folklore and performance, home invasion narratives, and Black horror's relationship to the Radical Black aesthetic, the examples I discuss in this article refuse to center one perspective (either the child or adult), and instead reflect on who has the right to be afraid, who has the cultural influence to tell stories, and how those stories might act as means for examining and processing trauma.

Visual examples of Black horror, including the television series *Lovecraft Country* (2020); the picture books *Wee Winnie Witch's Skinny* (2004) by Virginia Hamilton and Barry Moser and *Precious and the Boo Hag* (2005) by Patricia McKissack, Onawumi Jean Moss, and Kyrsten Brooker; and the film *Us* (2019), recenter Black child subjectivity from images of the body in pain onto community belonging by challenging both the audience and subject divides between the child and adult. Films, television, and picture books offer experiences that are pleasurable to specific readers/viewers, but also invite families to experience media together, taking part as one interpretive community, and assigning intentions to the text (Fish 483). Visual media enmesh the reader/viewer in symbols, allowing different levels of reading and interpretation based on cultural knowledge.

Black horror makes intentional use of multi-layered visual symbolism, as Melba Boyd makes clear in her discussion of *Get Out*. Boyd examines the role of visual symbols such as deer heads, cotton, and tea cups, as well as parallels to *Guess Who's Coming to Dinner* (1967) and *The Matrix* (1999) to demonstrate that "layered duality is established in the opening scenes and is ingrained throughout the film's construct" (Boyd 37).[1] The layered semiotic construction of visual texts such as horror films and picture books allow for multiple accurate readings within an intended intergenerational audience.

Visual representations of children in horror reveal the politics of race, specifically what types of bodies have access to the cultural protections of childhood. Because it resists closure and violates boundaries, horror is a perfect medium to examine the breakdown of the divide between children and adults, as well as the role race plays in constructing that divide. When horror films and television from *Interview With a Vampire* to *The Walking Dead* wish to shock the audience by making a child character monstrous, those films and television shows rely on the white child, especially the white girl child, as the cultural embodiment of innocence. The reliance on white bodies for the perversion-of-innocence trope is in part because, as numerous scholars including Robin Bernstein have explained, Black children in white cultural spaces are rarely imagined as innocent. Bernstein observes that as innocence came to define childhood in the nineteenth century, innocence, and therefore childhood, was stripped from cultural depictions of Black children (Bernstein 34). In contrast to the angelic white child, Bernstein notes, Black children such as Topsy are depicted as "subhuman [. . .] merrily accepting (or even inviting) violence," and do not sustain injury or feel pain (34-36). Therefore, Bernstein argues that while the adult/child dichotomy exists in white representations of Black subjects, it exists in terms of a fetishization of pain: the Black adult is always a body in pain, the Black child incapable of pain (36). This focus on pain also means that Black children are viewed as adults much earlier than white children.

Child characters in Black horror interact with the monstrous as a means of resistance to racist violence. In her preface to *Horror Noire: Blacks in American Horror Films From the 1890s to the Present*, Robin Coleman recounts her own intergenerational experience with horror cinema: "I saw *Dawn of the Dead* with my grandmother and mother at the great Pittsburgh drive-in theater" (Coleman xvi). Coleman describes this viewing as a formative experience and goes on to explore the role of horror in illuminating cultural definitions of Blackness. The examples in this article (*Lovecraft Country, Wee Winnie Witch's Skinny, Precious and the Boo Hag,* and *Us*) build on Coleman's thesis through the use of home invasion narratives, centering the Black home and family.[2] These examples acknowledge that threats to Black subjectivity are continuous, but the family remains, grows, and passes on art and love to the next generation. From James Lee telling the story of Wee Winnie Witch to his grandchild to *Lovecraft Country's* ghostly matriarchs saving their descendants from a racist cult, these stories emphasize the protection, love, and wisdom of family. I argue that this bringing-together of adults, children, families, and neighbors carries a powerful message of belonging and value as its own Radical Aesthetic within Black horror.

Black horror presents children as powerful, invites adults to assume the roles of children within the story, and aligns adults and children together against a monstrous outside force. In order to create this sense of community, however, the genre must begin with the fundamental question that both Kinitra Brooks and Robin Coleman ask in their respective manuscripts: what is the role of the Black character within horror? In their discussion of *Candyman* (1992), Aviva Briefel and Sianne Ngai phrase this differently: "The struggle we see in the horror film is not only a struggle over property, but a struggle over who has the right to be afraid" (Briefel and Ngai 72). Briefel and Ngai align this "right to be afraid" with property ownership, specifically the divide in *Candyman* (1992) between the white academics who live in upscale condos and the Black families in the Cabrini-Green housing projects. Brooks and Coleman independently argue that Black characters in horror have only recently acquired the right to be afraid, and to have their fear taken seriously by the narrative. The shift that Black characters in horror experience—from objects to subjects—parallels the narrative shift of Topsy from an object of white ridicule to a subject of Black horror and draws attention to the role of the Black child within the genre. Since Black children have been historically marginalized and abused within horror, their role offers a specific point of entry to investigate the genre's evolving depictions of Black pain, both physical and psychological, as well as changing depictions of Black communities.

Intergenerational Protection and Community

Black horror texts and media such as *Lovecraft Country* juxtapose the visual narrative perspectives of adults and children to highlight both the monstrousness of racist violence, and the reparative aspects of family and community. *Lovecraft Country* follows Atticus "Tic" Freeman, along with his girlfriend, father, aunt, uncle, and cousins as they battle a white supremacist cult called the Sons of Adam. The cult kidnaps Tic's father and lures Tic to an estate where they plan to sacrifice him to achieve immortality. When the sacrifice fails and the Freemans escape, cult members across the country vow revenge. The entire family is at risk, and so they come together across space and time to defeat the cult.

While all of *Lovecraft Country* communicates the importance of family and community in the face of racist violence, the Tulsa episode in particular illustrates a few key factors regarding the role of children in Black horror. In episode 8 of the series, Diana Freeman runs away from her friend Emmett Till's funeral and is cursed by a cult leader. In episode 9, to save Diana from the curse, Diana's mother, uncle, and cousin go back in time to the Tulsa Massacre and reclaim the magic that is their family legacy.

The Tulsa episode highlights both the vulnerability of children, and their necessary role within the larger Black community. First, children are just as threatened by the monster of racist violence as adults are and must fight against it. Diana is not helpless in the face of this violence. She funnels Topsy and Bopsy into a bottleneck and hits them with a lead pipe, but they scratch her anyway (Green "Jig-A-Bobo"). Diana demonstrates that children are not exempt from racism because of their age, and that they can be formidable in the fight against that violence, but even then, they might lose. While Diana's struggle against the twins is fiction, Emmett Till's death haunts the episode, reminding the audience that the threat of violence against Black childhood is very real.

Second, the past informs the present. Atticus and Diana Freeman have access to magic because of their ancestor Hanna's escape from slavery. Atticus must experience the violence of Tulsa in order to reclaim that magic. The sins of the past continue into the present in the form of racist policing systems that harm Diana, but knowledge of the past is vital for healing and protecting the Black family. Despite a school system that largely omits both the violence done to Black bodies and the role of Black labor in building the United States, Black horror shows how knowing the past is a necessary step to curbing racist violence in both personal and institutional settings.

Third, even after the immediate threat is neutralized, Diana will always live with scars. Whether these scars are the psychological toll of her friend Emmett Till's death, the cultural scars of figures like Topsy shaping depictions of Black childhood, or the physical scars of losing her right arm, surviving does not mean that Black children do not bear lasting effects from racist violence. Black horror may act as a means of processing the scars left by racism and the continuation of racist institutions, but it also acts as a clarion call to protect Black personhood and Black childhood by re-centering representations of Black identity around community belonging and support, rather than depictions of the body in pain.

Finally, family and community are necessary for survival. No one member of the family can survive alone. They all must help one another and accept help when they need it. Though the Freeman family has its own internal prejudices and arguments, they have to come together to face the monsters outside. Each member of the family has their own unique trauma to process brought on by factors such as gender, sexuality, military service, and so on. These characters are not monolithic in their experience of or response to white violence, but they do support one another.

At the end of Matt Ruff's novel, on which the television series is based, Atticus strips cult leader Caleb Braithwaite's powers. The white man threatens, "It's Not Over! There are other lodges, all over America, and they know about you, now. [. . .] They won't think of you as family, or even as a person, And they won't leave you alone until they get what they want from you. No matter where you go, you'll never be safe" (Ruff 365). Caleb stops speaking as every Black character assembled erupts into laughter, and Atticus explains, "What is it you're trying to scare me with? You think I don't know what country I live in? I know. We all do. We always have. You're the one who doesn't understand" (Ruff 366). What the white villains in *Lovecraft Country* do not understand is that being Black in America already means existing in a constant state of danger, whether that existence is in 1954 or 2021. The aesthetic project of Black horror is to name that danger and present its characters with opportunities to navigate or defeat it. For Black children, both inside and outside the media or text, this imaginative opportunity to push back against racist violence, to "envision an alternative world or future," is the first step to making it reality (Schalk 2). I return to *Lovecraft Country*'s role in evolving depictions of Black horror, specifically depictions of home invasion, later in the article.

As *Lovecraft Country* demonstrates, Black horror in visual media allows the reader/viewer multiple subject positions and invites various levels of reading, creating interpretive space for an intentionally wide audience that includes both children and adults, and drawing attention to the subversive role of child characters. These levels of reading are not stratified, but rather open to every reader/viewer based on cultural knowledge. The same reader/viewer can then return to a work, accessing new parts of the work each time and increasing both their appreciation for it, as well as their overall knowledge and ability to read and interpret other works. In this way all visual texts are, as Perry Nodelman claims, didactic, but this didacticism is not limited to a child audience. Nodelman explains how picture books, like film, appear to grant a position of authority to the reader/viewer since "they exist only so that we can look at them" (75). Nodelman discusses the semiotics of illustration, calling picture books "particularly powerful deceivers" because they purport to clearly and accurately represent the world outside the text while "integrat[ing] young children into the ideology of our culture" (Nodelman 72-73). Nodelman points out that at the same time that they seem to place the reader in a position of "uninvolved egocentric observation," illustrations also constrain the reader by requiring that they accept certain cultural symbols in order to make meaning (76).

In contrast to Nodelman's observation, visual media can also work to create empathy between the character and the reader/viewer. Susanna Hoeness-Krupsaw argues that graphic representations enhance the experience for the reader, creating a greater empathy for the character through facial expressions, body language, color, and composition (Hoeness-Krupsaw 119-128). Martha Cutter looks to illustrated anti-slavery texts for evidence that illustration can "move a reader beyond spectator mode of parallel empathy that entails vicarious introspection" (Cutter 224). Carol Clover points out that sensational or "body genres" such as horror and pornography, in which bodies appear in the throes of extreme emotion, elicit a physical reaction in the viewer similar to what the character is experiencing (Clover 189). For each of these scholars, the visual aspects of media are essential for both making meaning and for building reader/viewer empathy. In fact, because horror is a body genre, visual texts invite the reader/viewer to experience the same psycho-physiological responses as the character, generating embodied empathy between a child viewer and adult character or an adult reader and child character.

Wee Winnie Witch's Skinny, Precious and the Boo Hag, the third episode of *Lovecraft Country*, and the film *Us* are all examples of home invasion narratives, and this subgenre uses visual elements to move the audience's perspective between characters, building a connection between the audience and multiple subject positions, including both adult and child characters. Home invasion narratives also highlight the importance of community as the featured family must help one another and work through any internal conflicts in order to survive. Home invasion narratives also reflect the shift in Black horror into the suburbs. For example, in 1995, demolition and gentrification began on Chicago's Cabrini-Green housing project, the setting of the original *Candyman* (1992). The last high-rise was demolished in 2011. A *Candyman* set in 2020 cannot occur in Cabrini-Green, since the housing project no longer stands. While housing discrimination and poverty are major themes in *Candyman*, where the Black characters are victims or monsters, contemporary Black horror branches out into the suburbs, recasting Black characters (now property owners) as heroes and dealing more explicitly, as Kinitra Brooks notes, with the concerns of middle-class Black families.

Contemporary horror, in recasting Black characters as the heroes, relocates Black identity formation from a focus on pain (poverty, poor housing, drugs, and gang violence in 1992's *Candyman*) to the survival of family and community. According to these contemporary examples, Black horror takes the position that Black people have a right to fear for themselves and their families in the face of racist institutions and violence. These Black families, especially Black children, can be the heroes, the protectors rather than the victims or monsters that white horror often portrays them as.

Black Folklore and Performance

Black horror also highlights the role of the community via folklore, whether the imagined urban legend of *Us*, the one-hundred-year-old mise-en-scène of Lovecraftian horrors, or the Gullah legend of the Boo Hag. In *Searching for Sycorax: Black Women's Hauntings of Contemporary Horror*, Kinitra D. Brooks coins the term "folkloric horror" which she defines as "a mix of African tradition, horror, fantasy, and science fiction elements created and employed by black women creatives" (Brooks 98). For Brooks, who begins her book by talking about a childhood experience with horror (watching *Vamp* in theaters with her aunt when she was seven), folkloric horror is a particularly useful structure to explore the "rich potential for the horror genre to successfully examine the social anxieties that often plague contemporary middle-class black women" (Brooks ix, 96). Indeed, the expanding cultural recognition of the Black middle class is changing the role of familial Black subjects within big-budget horror films and highlighting the transformative roles of Black children. Brooks reads folkloric horror as active or performative, an extension of the conjure woman. Authors and singers might weave a song or story in the same way their forebearers wove spells. Brooks describes Nina Simone's "I Put a Spell on You" in just this way (Brooks 124-125).

Thinking about visual media as a form of conjure performance, I argue, is useful in examining the role that Black women in particular play in protecting their families, and how these acts of protection make new space for Black childhood. Brooks's folkloric horror also suggests that these books, films, and shows themselves are a form of protective magic. This performance of intergenerational cooperation and protection casts the reader/viewer as a child in order to ward them against racist violence. This use of performance is perhaps most clear in picture books, intended to be read aloud by an adult to a child audience.

Both *Precious and the Boo Hag* and *Wee Winnie Witch's Skinny* invite a reader/audience relationship that mirrors the community depicted in the text as the protective spells or songs are read aloud.

Written by Newbery Honor-, NAACP Image Award-, and Coretta Scott King Award-winner Patricia McKissak and storyteller Onawumi Jean Moss, *Precious and the Boo Hag* details Pruella the Boo Hag's attempts to get inside Precious's house when Precious's mother is away. Pruella can make herself look like anything, and so Precious must be calm and outsmart her. The advice that Precious's mother gives her allows Precious to protect herself and her home from the witchy invader. Similarly, Virginia Hamilton's *Wee Winnie Witch's Skinny,* subtitled "An Original African American Scare Tale," tells the story of James Lee and his Uncle Anthony's encounter with a witch.[4] The witch removes her skin to ride Uncle Anthony, flying him through the night using a bridle made of his hair. Like Precious's mother, James Lee's Mama Granny knows all about witches. She puts hot sauce into the witch's skin so that when the witch puts it back on, it squeezes her until she falls to pieces. Both books allow a child protagonist to confront monstrosity directly with the support of maternal family members.

Precious's resistance to the Boo Hag depends on her mother's advice at the beginning of the text and reinforces both the importance of community and the role of children in resistance to monstrosity and violence. Despite the Boo Hag appearing in several different guises, including a child, an old woman, and a penny, Precious recognizes her each time and sings "Pruella is a Boo Hag—she's right outside my window. She's tricky and she's scary, but I won't let her in!" Precious's song acts as a spell, a performance that protects her from those who would do her harm (McKissack and Onawumi 13). The reader has to enact Precious's song while reading the book, and this reading (in addition to protecting readers from Boo Hags) illustrates the role of art and music as spaces of Black community resistance to violence. After Pruella is defeated, the book ends with another monster waiting outside Precious's room disguised as a tree, suggesting that Precious must continue to protect herself (40). The threats that await Black children are not limited to one encounter with a witch but require constant vigilance.

In *Wee Winnie*, the child James Lee and Mama Granny, the matriarch of the family, embody different and complementary forms of power. Page 18 of the text features a woodcut image of James Lee and Wee Winnie Witch riding Uncle Anthony. Text on the facing page describes the flight as well as Mama Granny's entrance into the house to find the witch's skin. At the same moment the child character is enjoying his ride, Mama Granny is bringing an end to the witch. By positioning the text that describes Mama Granny's arrival opposite the image of James Lee, the book refuses to prioritize one narrative over the other. James Lee's experience of the night ride occupies the same importance and space as Mama Granny's power over the witch. The next page features a woodcut of Mama Granny stirring her spice-hot pepper oil, sparking with orange flames and white stars. The reader/viewer can see Mama Granny's power in her determined facial expression and no-nonsense approach to witches. The reader is invited into the narratives of both James Lee and Mama Granny, simultaneously delighted and frightened by the picture book.

The book further breaks down the adult/child dichotomy in the last page, featuring an elderly James Lee telling the story to a young child on his lap. Illustrations of James Lee's storytelling begin and end the book. This last image mirrors the first one, in which James Lee is drawing a picture of a cat and telling his brother Will everything that he knows about witches. Although the book is written in third person, James Lee is the primary storyteller. In this way the reader experiences the transition from a child to an adult perspective over the course of the text, dismantling the child/adult divide and reinforcing both James Lee's evolving place in the family and the endurance of the family and community in spite of external threats.

These books highlight the importance of storytelling for passing on Black culture and traditions, in the same way that *Lovecraft Country* highlights the importance of passing on Black history. Academic as well as popular culture discussions should acknowledge the role of Black children's art as an essential part of horror and speculative fiction, the Radical Black Aesthetic, and protest more broadly conceived. Despite a lack of critical attention to the books, as picture books are not often included in discussions of horror, levels of understanding depicted in the texts include not only the basic story, but also the larger traditions of Black folklore, woodcut art, the Gullah stories surrounding Boo Hags, and the condition of sleep paralysis and its relationship to witch-riding and Black health.[5] While none of this information is necessary to a basic reading of the book, additional cultural or historical knowledge and background can deepen and change an individual appreciation of the story and alter how a reader experiences the text's horror. The Boo Hag might be a literal villain, a personification of a nameless evil from long-told stories, or a medical condition exacerbated by structural racism. Yet, despite how real the Boo Hag may be for the reader, the visceral experience of fear the text provokes for its child character and then relieves through family support emphasizes both the importance of Black children within the community, and the strength of the intergenerational community in the face of horror.[6]

Showrunner Misha Green enacts a similar form of performance as catharsis and protective magic at the end of season 1, episode 2 of *Lovecraft Country*, "Whitey on the Moon". Reviews of the series focus on how Green "finds ways to link the horrors the characters face with the everyday horrors of Black life" (Hale). Similarly, Matt Ruff's novel focuses on Black parents' inability to consistently protect their children, as the character Montrose Turner explains, "He had this look on his face. Horror. Horror at the universe. [...] That's the horror, the most awful thing: to have a child the world wants to destroy and know that you're helpless to help him. Nothing worse than that. Nothing worse" (Ruff 293-294). In the show, parents protect their children through magic, opening space for Black childhood to directly confront the monstrous. In episode 2, Tic Freeman (Jonathan Majors) is forced to participate in an occult ceremony that will kill him in order to give the white cult members eternal life. During the ceremony, Gil-Scott Heron's "Whitey's on the Moon" plays in place of a musical score. The poem reminds the audience of how Tic's current position as a sacrifice to white overreach is part of a much longer history of similar actions. As Heron ends the poem "I think I'll send these doctor bills air-mail special to Whitey on the moon," Tic's ancestor Hanna appears in a portal and Tic reaches out to her (Green "Whitey's On The Moon").

In this scene, not only does the poem act as an incantation, replacing for the viewer whatever the cult would be chanting in this moment; it is also a prelude to the real magic. Hanna (Joaquina Kalukango) appears, turning the cult members to stone and guiding Tic to safety. He is able to flee the house just as she did, while the entire structure collapses. Hanna's presence suggests that she is protecting Tic, an incarnation of the folkloric conjure woman Brooks describes. It is unclear in this sequence how Hanna achieves this power, but the show seems to suggest that her addition to Tic's bloodline marks him as unique and different from the white cult members. Her presence guides and protects him in a way that his white ancestors do not. Hanna helps Tic survive so that he in turn can protect his young cousin Diana, freeing her from Topsy and Bopsy's curse. Diana then kills Christina Braithwhite, the cult member pursuing Tic and his family. In this way, performed protection magic cycles through the family from adult to child, creating a circle that includes family, both living and dead, in an inheritance of Black survival and support.

Precious, James Lee, and Tic all engage directly with the monstrous and are saved by a parent or ancestor. Although Tic is not a child per se, his role as Hanna's descendant places him in a position of helplessness compared to the women who save and protect him. Similarly, Precious relies on her mother's advice to protect her from Pruella, and James Lee relies on his grandmother. These protagonists are agentic but not self-sufficient, and as the implications of familial belonging are reinforced, the divide between child and adult is broken down: children are allowed to confront the monstrous directly, and adults are constantly reminded that they are someone else's child and worthy of protection.

By allowing everyone—including adult men, veterans, and heroes—the protections of childhood, Black horror challenges the exclusion of Black children from white cultural spaces. By having ancestors or parental figures come to the aid of Tic, James Lee, and Precious, these stories use folklore, performance, and visual symbols to invoke the cultural power of Black communities to protect their members against outside threats including racist violence, refocusing narrative closure from the sources of terror and trauma to the strategies for protection and repair. These stories speak directly to white horror which often casts the Black body as a threat, realigning monstrosity with white supremacy and making Black characters the heroes of their own stories.

The Home Invasion Narrative

Unlike *Wee Winnie Witch's Skinny, Precious and the Boo Hag,* or *Lovecraft Country,* however, Jordan Peele's *Us* does not require an adult to save the children the film endangers, but rather has them save themselves by stealing identities, becoming the leaders of a rebellion, killing their evil twins, or acknowledging their mother's true identity and choosing how to act. Home invasion narratives such as *Us* conclude with a restoration of safety within the family rather than the physical space of the home. Throughout the story, the characters learn about themselves and what they are capable of while strengthening their familial bonds.

In *Us*, Adelaide Thomas (Lupita Nyong'o) wanders into a funhouse as a child and meets someone who looks exactly like her. As an adult, she and her family visit the same area on vacation, and the first night are confronted with doppelganger home invaders. The family learns that a secret underground government experiment has created these soulless doubles, the Tethered, who are choosing to rise up and kill their twins. Adelaide and her family kill their doubles, until Adelaide's double, Red, kidnaps the family's young son and takes him underground. Red and Adelaide fight, and the audience learns that Adelaide is the Tethered who replaced Red as a child. Adelaide kills Red, saves her son, and returns to the surface as the family escapes and the camera pans out to reveal thousands of Tethered holding hands. Although the film does not take place entirely within the physical space of the home, it retains the elements of a home invasion narrative.

While the film does not focus on the Tethereds' backstory or the reasons for their existence, the larger role of the Tethered within the story is to dramatize the similarity between the monstrous underclass and the respectable middle-class family. Red and Adelaide appear identical. They are so similar, in fact, that when Adelaide's parents take Red home by mistake, they never suspect that the child living with them is not their daughter. What separates Red and Adelaide, or in fact the oppressed and therefore monstrous, soulless, and violent Tethered from the family centered in the narrative is mere luck. The film demonstrates that the centered family are not less violent than the Tethered as they are capable of murder in their own defense. Nor is the middle-class family different from the Tethered in any meaningful way other than their upbringing and access to the resources of the world above. Thus, one of the major sources of horror in the film is not simply the Tethereds' invasion of Adelaide's (or by extension the audience's) home and life, but the fact that

Adelaide (or the audience) is in fact a Tethered and could be dragged back into that state at any time. The horror of *Us* is not just the home invasion, but the constant American proximity to poverty.

Home invasion narratives focus on the "right to be afraid." In these stories, a monstrous other threatens the safety of the protagonists' home and family, a reversal, Coleman argues, of 1930s horror in which the (coded Black) monsters invade the white home and family.[6] As Dario Marcuccio points out, "Invaders mirror the inner crisis of the family, and the invasion uncovers buried tensions and grief" (Marcuccio 257). Similar to *Lovecraft Country*, *Us* sparks "a moment of growing recognition that the deeds of the past still rage with silent and devastating force in the present time" in a way that is "intrinsically political, even revolutionary" (Brody). Harry Olafsen reads the film in context of Homi Bhaba's mimicry, concluding that "coming face-to-face with the Other—an Other that looks identical—produces fear, anxiety, and horror" but that "dual nature of mimicry means that 'the soul remains one'" (Olafsen 30). These doubles could also be read as examples of Du Bois's double-consciousness, as the main characters appear as both a middle-class family and members of the oppressed underclass.

Us switches back and forth between child and adult perspectives throughout the film, and, I argue, refuses to privilege one narrative perspective over the other. First, *Us* allows the children to kill their own Tethered, making them heroes in their own right rather than victims to be protected. The camera even follows the children rather than staying focused on Adelaide, giving the audience their narrative perspectives as well. Secondly, the film flashes back in time, mixing and slipping between the child and adult Adelaide and provoking embodied viewer empathy for both perspectives. The film takes pains to both reinforce the child-like qualities of these characters and to point out how violence affects them. *Us* reimagines Black childhood as both liberating and empowering, cared for and capable, safe and strong. The film emphasizes the child identities of characters while also acknowledging the realities of Black children who must be able to defend themselves against racist cultural systems.

In the film, the two children kill their Tethered in ways that mimic the Tethereds' attacks on them. More interestingly, just like *Wee Winnie* or *Precious and the Boo Hag*'s refusal to elevate the adult narrative perspective over the child's, the camera aligns the audience with the child subjects rather than focusing on Adelaide or making the children seem small or vulnerable. Zora (Shahadi Wright Joseph) is a teenaged track star whose Tethered, Umbrae, chases her when Red tells her to "run." The camera stays on Zora as the two girls mirror one another on opposite sides of a parked car. Umbrae disappears and the camera follows Zora as she bends down to look under the car. Zora is visibly frightened, breathing quickly and with wide eyes, physical symptoms that might be mirrored by the audience as the camera angle alternately aligns them with Zora's perspective (often just behind her head) and shows her facial expressions. When Umbrae is distracted, Zora runs away to rejoin her family. At the neighbors' house, Zora and her younger brother Jason (Evan Alex) kill several Tethered with a golf club and a statue. The camera, again, alternates between the children's perspectives, often just behind their heads, and shots of their faces and body language so that the audience can both see what they see and how it affects them.

The film not only takes the children's perspectives, but also makes them just as formidable as the adults. When the family escapes, Zora argues that she should drive because "I have the highest kill count in the family." Adelaide says that no, she killed the second twin and Jason jumps in with, "I killed Kitty." Their father Gabe reiterates, "So that's one, one, one, and two. I killed two. I killed myself and Josh, so…" (Peele). Yet, Zora immediately ups her kill count by running over Umbrae, who charges the car. Much of the camerawork in this scene focuses on Zora, despite the entire family being in the car. Again, the camera cuts between her face and her perspective. At this point in the film, the children are just as capable of taking out the Tethered as their parents are. In the next scene, Jason's Tethered, Pluto, threatens the family with fire and Adelaide reaches out to him because Pluto is her son (sort of). Jason walks him backward into the fire, killing him. Unlike previous scenes, this one alternates between Adelaide's perspective and Jason's, so that rather than identifying purely with the child, the audience also sees a mother's pain at losing her son, a necessary precursor to the final act when Jason is kidnapped.

The camera work does not linger on either the children's or the Tethered's injuries or pain, choosing to highlight instead familial bonds. It does so by grouping subjects together in wide shots, focusing on the emotional reactions to violence rather than physical ones with close-ups of the character's faces, and having the family reunite after each violent incident, visibly happy to see one another. These moments in the film challenge traditional distinctions between children and adults that rely on notions of competence. Zora's argument that she should be able to drive because of her kill count, and Jason figuring out before anyone else what Pluto's plan is, demonstrate the capability of children. Zora and Jason end the movie with the same number of kills as their parents, suggesting that every member of the family is equally formidable as a horror film hero, and that Black bodies, regardless of age, face violent threats in American society. The children are not relegated to watching the action or being protected while their parents fight. Jason and Zora are just as heroic as their parents, and their Tethered counterparts are just as monstrous. Umbrae and Pluto try to murder the family multiple times, making them as threatening as Red. While the film does not position the viewer to identify with the Tethered children, it does afford them the same level of power as the adults, suggesting that good or bad, young people are deserving of being the center of the narrative.

In the final sequence of the film, when Red kidnaps Jason and takes him underground, she uses the opportunity to flash back to her childhood and explain to Adelaide how she staged the uprising. Red makes paper dolls, a childish method of explaining her plan. The film backtracks to the day the two girls met and walks viewers through the detritus of Red's childhood while explaining how the two women are connected, with Red telling Adelaide, "I never stopped thinking about you. You could have taken me with you." The film jumps back and forth between present day Red and Adelaide fighting, and their child versions dancing, splicing past and present together in terms of choreography and meaning. The score for this scene is an orchestral arrangement of Luniz's "I Got 5 on It," a song that the family sings along to in the car earlier in the film in a moment of bonding and to defuse familial tension. Not only does the song support the film's use of doubling, but it also heightens the audience experience of being displaced in time, circling back to both Adelaide's and Red's childhoods and an earlier moment in the film.

After Adelaide kills Red and saves Jason, returning to the surface, the film ends with an extended flashback sequence explaining how Adelaide replaced Red, learned to speak, and assumed her life. While this reveal circumvents narrative closure (as does a final helicopter shot of the Tethered), it also pulls Adelaide back into her childhood self; although killing Red may have ended the immediate threat, it did not comfort the child Adelaide who is still afraid that she will be found out. The camera pans from Adelaide's face to a close up on Jason, suggesting that he may know the truth. Here the child Jason takes the place of the adult Red as the keeper of Adelaide's secret. The film slips between the adult and child versions of the same character as the subject of narrative focus and audience empathy. In this way, not only does *Us* allow the viewer into the child character's perspective, but also casts the adult character as a child, emphasizing the role of Black children within the community.

The Radical Black Aesthetic

Black horror acknowledges the humanity of Black children, their ability to feel physical and emotional pain, and the legitimacy of their fears, recentering Black subjectivity not around pain, but the survival of the community and familial relationships. Horror as a genre gives physical shape to cultural fears. In white horror, that fear is often depicted as universal, yet is actually specific to an imagined invasion of middle-class white spaces, communities, or reproductive networks. In contrast, Black horror wrestles with the emotional and historical toll of Black pain while also claiming space for Black communities and families and investing in an aesthetic of liberation. The intergenerational family in horror can act as a confining force, a microcosm of state power. In his *Hearths of Darkness*, Tony Williams outlines specific instances in which the family becomes a source of horror by torturing and perverting its members into submission, such as *Psycho* (1960) or *The Texas Chainsaw Massacre* (1974) (Williams). Yet, family can also be empowering and supportive, as in the home invasion film. As Catharine Lester points out, horror that includes "independent, resourceful, and identifiable [child] characters who do not need the help of adults" may be especially appealing to intergenerational audiences (Lester 34). I argue that unlike narratives that focus on Black pain or use the family as a source of horror, contemporary Black horror featuring multi-generational families centers on relationships that empower Black children, preparing them to resist racist violence and allowing these characters to become sites of cultural resistance both inside and outside of the text or film.

Black horror calls for accountability for racist violence. John Jennings's visual essay "Scratching at the Dark" describes Black horror, or what he terms the ethno-gothic, as an exploration of a "haunted" Black experience in an America uninterested in dealing with the "negative effects of racial discrimination which still affect Black people every day in nearly every facet of society" (Jennings 251).[7] He continues, "So we make stories to hold the pain" (Jennings 251). For authors and scholars including Jennings, Ryan Poll, Robin Coleman, and Tananarive Due, the Radical Aesthetic of Black horror represents what has been, as well as what is possible, by calling for an accounting from white violence, but not allowing whiteness to define the narrative. For example, *Lovecraft Country* dramatizes sundown towns, slavery, racial profiling, rough rides, redlining and pioneering, the death of Emmett Till, the Tulsa massacre, medical experimentation, kidnapping, cross burning, and the destruction of Black-friendly businesses. Much of the horror and tension in *Lovecraft Country* (and Black horror more generally) does not come from the ghosts or monsters, but from the daily racist threats the characters face, which even when set in the past, reflect contemporary struggles. These stories act as repositories of tensions and fears, since as Jennings points out, "a ghost is just trauma with a shape" (Jennings 252).

As part of the larger category of speculative fiction, horror also works as a mode of artistic resistance to existing racial and adult-centered power structures. As Sami Schalk points out, "Speculative fiction allows us to imagine otherwise, to envision an alternative world or future" and "For marginalized people, this can mean imagining a future or alternative space away from oppression or in which relations between currently empowered and disempowered groups or altered or improved" (Schalk 2). Despite a larger cultural binary of mature/immature subjects which seeks to limit children's exposure to adult topics such as sexuality and violence, Coleman notes that horror "prides itself on snuggling up next to the taboo" (13), and so is willing to put children in danger, or even cast children as monsters. Horror ignores or intentionally violates cultural protections for children, offering its child protagonists as possible points of identification for adult audiences, and inviting child audience members to see themselves as powerful.

Contemporary Black horror, as an example of what Reynaldo Anderson terms the Black Speculative Arts Movement, is a form of protest that re-centers Black child subjectivity not on the fetishization of Black pain, but on the individual-within-community's ability to thrive in the face of white violence (Anderson). Ryan Poll argues that in *Get Out* (2017) "becoming and staying woke is, in large part, a project of aesthetics," specifically a Radical Black Aesthetic. This Radical Black Aesthetic may include the intersection between performance and politics that Fred Moten describes in *In The Break* (2003), or as Poll suggests, Afro-pessimism, which requires subjects to acknowledge the continued role of slavery in shaping Black identity in the US (Poll 80). Poll claims that Black aesthetics are a political project that calls white culture to account for the continued violence against Black bodies and identities from the advent of racialized slavery to the present. As Tananarive Due says, "Black history is Black horror" (Berlatsky). Black horror artists and scholars such as visual artist John Jennings build on this exploration of the Black Radical Aesthetic. Jennings speaks to the emergence of speculative media more broadly, including *Black Panther*, *Luke Cage*, and *Black Lightning* as aspects of Afrofuturism within a larger Black Speculative Arts Movement (Batiste, Boelcskevy, and Lewis 18).[8] Black horror is part of the larger Speculative Arts Movement that Jennings describes. In an interview with Noah Berlatsky, Jennings explains, "You know there's the Black Arts Movement, the Harlem Renaissance, this Black speculative arts movement that's happening right now. We fight with our art. We've always fought with our dance, and our music, and our paintings" (Berlatsky). Black horror draws together the community both inside and outside of the text, film, or television show to fight a monstrous incursion that often works as a metaphor for structural racism. In this fight for self-definition and community preservation, Black children play pivotal roles.

Remakes of *Candyman* and *The People Under the Stairs* suggest that the future of Black horror will continue to call for accountability for racist violence and will focus on reparative strategies for Black subjects and communities. Trailers and advertisements for Nia DaCosta's *Candyman* mix folklore with history to create images of both horror and protest. A black and white trailer for the film released on June 17, 2020 features puppets that are visually similar to Kara Walker's silhouettes. The trailer tells the story of a Black artist who paints portraits of Black people murdered by white violence. The trailer includes four stories, two that might reference Candyman, and two real ones— the lynching of James Byrd Jr. and the execution of George Stinney, Jr. Stinney's death as well as Walker's paintings illustrate threats to Black children. Walker paints exaggerated tableaux of slavery, highlighting cruelty and pain. Similarly, Stinney's death— at 14, making him the youngest person ever executed in the US—represents contemporary police shootings of Black young people.

DaCosta draws on folkloric horror to tell a story about violence against Black bodies and the psychic toll that violence takes on a community. As William Burke (Colman Domingo) in the live-action trailer explains, "Candyman is how we deal with the fact that these things happen. That they're still happening" ("Tell Everyone"). In these trailers, DaCosta and her actors ritualistically perform Black folkloric horror as catharsis, over-exaggerating elements of real-life horror so that they are easier to recognize and process. These trailers suggest that investment in Black horror is growing, and that future projects including *Candyman* (2021), *The People Under The Stairs*, *Nope*, and others will continue the Radical Black Aesthetic projects of fighting for cultural protections for Black children, and recentering Black subjectivity from spectacles of the body in pain onto positive portrayals of intergenerational families and communities as sites of reparative love and belonging.

Notes

1. Because *Get Out*'s cultural symbols are specific to a contemporary Black American experience, viewers outside of this group may have difficulty reading aspects of the film, as evidenced by the film's 2018 Golden Globe nomination for Best Comedy. This misreading of *Get Out* suggests that Black horror is primarily invested in Black viewers, prefacing their needs before those of other audience categories, such as awards committees.
2. The examples listed here include Black showrunners, directors, and majority Black casts.
3. Jessica McCort's *Reading in the Dark* offers a notable exception as the collection does read picture books as horror but does not address these particular texts.
4. Hamilton, like McKissak, has published multiple award-winning works of Black folklore for children. Hamilton's honors include the Hans Christian Andersen Award, the Children's Literature Legacy Award, the MacArthur Fellowship, the Edgar Allan Poe Award, the Coretta Scott King Award, the National Book Award and the Newbery Medal.
5. For more information on cultural traditions surrounding Boo Hags see Terrance Zepke's *Lowcountry Voodoo: Beginner's Guide to Tales, Spells and Boo Hags* (2009) and *Ghosts and Legends of the Carolina Coasts* (2005), Alan Brown's *Haunted*

South Carolina: Ghosts and Strange Phenomena of the Palmetto State (2010), and Henry Louis Gates and Maria Tatar's *The Annotated African American Folktales* (2017).

6. Coleman specifically mentions *Ingagi* (1930), *The Monster Walks* (1932), and *King Kong* (1933) as examples.

7. Jennings's title echoes Toni Morrison's *Playing in the Dark* (1992), which calls attention to the roles of Black figures within white-authored texts.

8. Afrofuturism uses science fiction and fantasy as gateways to reimagine both the past and the future for new avenues of Black liberation (Womack 2013, 7-9).

Works Cited

Anderson, Reynaldo. "Afrofuturism 2.0 & the Black Speculative Arts Movement: Notes on a Manifesto." *Obsidian,* vol. 42 no. 1-2, 2016, pp. 228-236.

Batiste, Stephanie L., Mary Anne Boelcskevy, and Shireen K. Lewis. "Interview with John Jennings, Featuring Alternate and Draft Panels from *Kindred: the Graphic Novel Adaptation*." *The Black Scholar,* vol. 48 no. 4, 2018, pp. 8-18.

Berlatsky, Noah. "Re-Centering the Black Experience in the Horror Genre, from *Beloved* to *Get Out*." *Document Journal,* 18 Aug. 2020, www.documentjournal.com/2020/06/re-centering-the-black-experience-in-the-horror-genre-from-beloved-to-get-out/.

Bernstein, Robin. *Racial Innocence: Performing American Childhood and Race From Slavery to Civil Rights*. Vol. 16. NYU Press, 2011.

Boyd, Melba Joyce. "Double Entendre and Double Consciousness in the Cinematic Construct of *Get Out*." *Black Renaissance/Renaissance Noire,* vol. 18, no. 3, 2018, pp. 36-44.

Briefel, Aviva, and Sianne Ngai. ""How Much Did You Pay For This Place?" Fear, Entitlement, and Urban Space in Bernard

Rose's *Candyman.*" *Camera Obscura: Feminism, Culture, and Media Studies,* vol. 13 no.1, 1996, pp. 69-91.

Brody, R. "Review: Jordan Peele's *Us* Is a Colossal Cinematic Achievement." *The New York Times.* 23 March 2019, https://www.newyorker.com/culture/the-front-row/review-jordan-peeles-us-is-a-colossal-cinematic-achievement

Brooks, Kinitra D. *Searching for Sycorax: Black Women's Hauntings of Contemporary Horror.* Rutgers University Press, 2018.

Candyman. "Paper" Trailer, 17 June 2020, Directed by Nia DeCosta. Metro-Gaolwyn-Mayer, Monkeypaw Productions, Bron Creative, https://www.youtube.com/watch?v=8-aieYI8L5I

Candyman. "Tell Everyone" Trailer, 29 June 2020, Directed by Nia DeCosta. Metro-Gaolwyn-Mayer, Monkeypaw Productions, Bron Creative, www.youtube.com/watch?v=kKXy31RV1bE

Clover, Carol J. "Her Body, Himself: Gender in the Slasher Film." *Representations,* vol. 20, 1987, pp. 187-228.

Coleman, Robin, R. Means. *Horror Noire: Blacks in American Horror Films from the 1890s to Present.* Taylor & Francis, 2011.

Cutter, Martha J. *The Illustrated Slave: Empathy, Graphic Narrative, and the Visual Culture of the Transatlantic Abolition Movement, 1800-1852.* University of Georgia Press, 2017.

Fish, Stanley E. "Interpreting the 'Variorum'." *Critical Inquiry,* vol. 2 no. 3, 1976, pp. 465-485.

Green, Misha. "Full Circle." *Lovecraft Country,* HBO, 18 Oct. 2020.

Green, Misha. "Jig-A-Bobo." *Lovecraft Country,* HBO, 4 Oct. 2020.

Green, Misha. "Whitey's On The Moon." *Lovecraft Country,* HBO, 23 Aug. 2020.

Hale, M. "*Lovecraft Country* Review: Nightmare on Jim Crow Street." *The New York Times,* 13 August 2020, https://www.nytimes.com/2020/08/13/arts/television/lovecraft-country-review.html

Hamilton, Virginia. *Wee Winnie Witch's Skinny: An Original African American Scare Tale.* Illustrated by Barry Moser. Blue Sky Press, 2004.

Hoeness-Krupsaw, Susanna. "8 Graphic Performances in Octavia Butler's *Kindred.*" *Performativity, Cultural Construction, and the Graphic Narrative,* edited by Leigh Anne Howard and Susanna Hoeness-Krupsaw, Routledge, 2019, pp. 118-132.

Jennings, John. "Scratching at the Dark: A Visual Essay on EthnoGothic." *Obsidian: Literature & Arts in the African Diaspora,* vol. 42 no. 1 & 2, 2017.

Lester, Catherine. "The Children's Horror Film: Characterizing an "Impossible" Subgenre." *The Velvet Light Trap,* vol. 78, 2016, pp. 22-37.

Marcucci, Dario. "Strangers at the Door: Space and Characters in Home Invasion Movies." *The Spaces and Places of Horror,* 2020, pp. 251-264.

McCort, Jessica R. "Introduction: Why horror? (Or, the importance of being frightened)." *Reading in the Dark: Horror in Children's Literature and Culture,* edited by Jessica R. McCort, UP of Mississippi, 2016, pp. 3-36.

McKissack, Pat, and Onawumi Jean Moss. *Precious and the Boo Hag.* Illustrated by Kyrsten Brooker. Simon and Schuster, 2005.

Morrison, Toni. *Playing in the Dark.* Vintage, 2007.

Moten, Fred. *In The Break: The Aesthetics of the Black Radical Tradition.* U of Minnesota Press, 2003.

Nodelman, Perry. "Decoding the Images: Illustration and Picture Books." *Understanding Children's Literature.* Routledge, 1998. pp. 79-90.

O'Loughlin, Jim. "Articulating *Uncle Tom's Cabin.*" *New Literary History,* vol. 31, no. 3, 2000, pp. 573-597.

Olafsen, Harry. "'It's Us:' Mimicry in Jordan Peele's *Us*." *Iowa Journal of Cultural Studies*, vol. 20 no.1, 2020, pp. 19-32.

Poll, Ryan. "'Can One *Get Out*?' The Aesthetics of Afro-Pessimism." *The Journal of the Midwest Modern Language Association*, vol. 51 no. 2, 2018, pp. 69-102.

Ruff, Matt. *Lovecraft Country*. Harper Collins, 2016.

Schalk, Sami. *Bodyminds Reimagined: (Dis) ability, Race, and Gender in Black Women's Speculative Fiction*. Duke University Press, 2018.

Stowe, Harriet Beecher. *Uncle Tom's Cabin*. Cosimo Classics, 2009.

Us. 2019. Directed by Jordan Peele. Universal Pictures.

Williams, Tony. *Hearths of Darkness: The Family in the American Horror Film*. Univ. Press of Mississippi, 2014.

Womack, Ytasha. *Afrofuturism: The World of Black Sci-fi and Fantasy Culture*. Chicago Review Press, 2013.

The Emotion of Dread in Cinematic Horror

Matthias De Bondt

IT IS UNDENIABLE THAT HORROR FILMS ARE "FELT" by their viewers. Recent research in Horror Studies has focused itself on this complex emotional experience, termed "affect," in the hope of gaining an understanding of the intricate dynamics of fictional fear. This article examines the research that has been conducted on affect in horror films. More specifically, it shines a light on the position that the emotion of dread, which has arguably been undertheorized, occupies within this discussion. Firstly, the article provides an overview of the literature and offers a critical analysis of the research that has been conducted on the emotion of dread. It asserts that such research has neglected the role that dread plays in the cinematic horror experience. In addition to this criticism, the article brings forward an expanded theoretical framework that leads to a more thorough insight into the affective experience of dread and the central place this emotion occupies within the cinematic horror experience. This theory is then put to the test through the close reading of two recent horror films, namely *It Comes At Night* and *The Blackcoat's Daughter*, both of which fall under what I term "dread-full films" – horror films that place the emotion of dread at the heart of their affective experience. The article will attend to pivotal scenes in these films while investigating the narrative and aesthetic elements necessary for eliciting the emotion of dread. Ultimately, the article wishes to reason that dread exists as an inseparable part of the viewing experience of these films and in doing so, argues that the emotion of dread is *inherent* to the overall cinematic horror experience.

Cognitive and phenomenological film theories[1]

Describing fear—whether it is real or fictional—is considered to be a difficult task. Fearful experiences are notoriously hard to communicate, and, like Elaine Scarry's description of pain, represent something "vaguely alarming yet unreal, loading with consequence yet evaporating before the mind" (Scarry 4). Fear, panic, horror, disgust: there are many overlapping words to describe such an experience, one of which is dread. In relation to the emotional experiences surrounding horror films, a first definition of dread is suggested by Noël Carroll, who describes the emotion in a Lovecraftian manner: "a sense of unease and awe, perhaps of momentary anxiety and foreboding ... to the point that one entertains the idea that unavowed, unknown, and perhaps concealed and inexplicable forces rule the universe" (42). Carroll differentiates real-life emotions from emotions evoked by aesthetic products such as films, calling them art-emotions instead. Art-dread, then, differs greatly from what Carroll considers to be the genre's main emotion, art-horror, which is propelled by the confrontation with the monstrous and constitutes Carroll's affective foundation for the horror film experience. His theory is therefore mainly entity-based: the monster – "a being in violation of the natural order" (40) – is seen as an inherent part of the cinematic experience and determines whether a film belongs to the genre or not. This stands in contrast to "tales of dread" (42), stories in which a lack of a definable monstrous threat is prominent. Carroll simply states that "art-dread probably deserves a theory of its own" (42), but pays no further attention to it.

Carroll's dismissal of dread is problematic as it clearly forms an important part of the emotional viewing experience of the horror genre. In fact, it is a crucial emotion in a number of horror films which I will describe here as "dread-full films." Contra Carroll, the affective-corporeal model of viewership as theorized by Xavier Aldana Reyes, mainly belonging to the cognitive-phenomenological approaches which have gained importance in film studies since the 1990s, offers a fuller consideration of the emotional dimensions of horror. While this article does not intend to conduct an in-depth investigation into the similarities and differences between film-phenomenology and cognitive film theory, some nuance is desirable to avoid further confusion. Film-phenomenologist Julian Hanich provides following clarification: "[w]hile the cognitivists try to explain why we feel certain emotions … phenomenology is interested in how we feel them" (*Cinematic Emotion* 13). In a nutshell, cognitive film theory, as described by David Bordwell, concerns itself with the cognitive and emotional reactions of viewers[2] to moving images ("Cognitive Theory"). Broadly speaking, as a theory, it aims to examine how narrative structures and aesthetic elements function in cinematic storytelling (Bordwell, *Narration*) and how spectators emotionally react to those images (Smith; Tan; Grodal; Plantinga). Phenomenology, instead, is "simply" about describing. The task of a phenomenological reading is "not to describe empirical and factual particulars, but to investigate the essential structures that characterize our experiences" (Zahavi 44). Phenomenologists uncover the structures of taken-for-granted phenomena and aim to arrive at their intrinsic "essence." Although there are several approaches out there, I limit myself here to the phenomenology as described by Maurice Merleau-Ponty. In contrast to Edmund Husserl's transcendental phenomenology, Merleau-Ponty argues that the universal essence of any phenomenon cannot be obtained without taking into account the embodied and lived experience associated with that particular phenomenon: "[t]he thing is inseparable from a person perceiving it, and can never really be actually in itself, because the articulations are those of our very existence" (373). Merleau-Ponty's ideas belong to the branch of existential phenomenology, that is, a phenomenology embedded in empirical existence. In cinema, Vivian Sobchack conceptualizes Merleau-Ponty's phenomenology as "a description of the film experience that includes the 'spectator' as well as the 'text' – that is, it ... calls for focus not only on elements of the film viewed but also on possible modes of engaging and viewing it" ("Phenomenology" 436). What phenomenology adds to the cinematic journey is the embodied viewing experience of a spectator. In doing so, cinematic spectatorship ends up on a spectrum in which the viewer's attention while watching a film continuously fluctuates between the film itself and his/her lived viewing experience.

The affective-corporeal model of viewership in horror

Reyes's affective-corporeal model originates from such a phenomenological background yet combines this with a cognitive approach. In his case studies, both film-aesthetic and narrative elements form the foundation for how a horror film affects its viewers. The phenomenological result of those elements, the outcome of textual cues on viewers, is expressed through the embodied viewing experience. Hence, one speaks of a cognitive-phenomenological model that examines both the film as an indicative text and the viewer as an embodied subject. Reyes distinguishes two possible responses one can have when reacting to these cues: cognitive (emotional) and corporeal (somatic) ones. The interaction between these two forms is not binary, but rather a complicated interplay that falls under the term "affect." According to Reyes, affect in Horror Studies is expressed in a universal way—namely "from a phenomenological point of view and thus taken ... at its emotional and somatic levels" (5). Reyes positions affect in our daily experiences and feelings: between cognitive emotions on the one hand and the somatic responses on the other, enabling a dynamic interaction between the two. Affect, quite simply, is that which viewers feel when watching a horror film, whether this feeling is mostly somatic (like the startle effect) or mostly cognitive (like the emotion of dread).

Building on the work of Carroll, Reyes encounters some limitations within his theory: "Carroll's theorization of art-horror, and perhaps the most controversial and problematic of his propositions, is that the formal object of emotion of art-horror are monsters" (91). Unclean creatures transgressing biological and cultural norms terrify both characters and viewers. Viewers do not necessarily believe that these monsters exist but rather play with the idea of their potential existence (Carroll 88). As Aaron Smuts states, "the thought theory is an incredibly intuitive, high-level account of how it is possible to be moved by fiction" (508). However, within Reyes's model, which focuses primarily on the emotional and somatic responses of spectators, Carroll's thought theory does not function as the centripetal force around which the genre operates. He therefore proposes a new theoretical paradigm, one that shifts from a monster-centered to a victim-centered point-of-view: "[h]orror is premised on the emotion of threat, an emotion that is often, but not exclusively, shared via imagination and somatic empathy with intradiegetic characters and, most importantly, their bodies" (97). The monster therefore only functions as a conduit that can be replaced by numerous malicious forces that are considered dangerous by spectators.

For Reyes, threat is the exclusive genre-defining state of horror: "[p]hysical threat lies at the heart of the horror experience and, where it is not working at a purely somatic level, it is necessarily connected to concomitant threat-processing cognitive and emotional states that come together to generate what we call fear" (104). The threat theory works on three levels: representative, by means of the frequent presence of "images of abjection" (58); emotional, "to create an emotional-affective canvas" (134) in which fear of/by characters is aroused in the presence of a threat; and somatic, as part of "viewer's engagement with the bodies on the screen" (186). It should be noted that the threats mentioned by Reyes are always highly specific and well-defined, ranging from demonic zombies in Balagueró and Plaza's *[•REC]* to gruesome torture objects in Wan's *Saw*. While no boundary-crossing monster needs to be present, danger materializes time and again in prototypical situations that are considered to be life-threatening in everyday life or the story-world of the film.

Reyes's theory is therefore extremely well suited for horror films in which visceral and graphic horrors play a major role but lacks certain strength when applied to horror films that primarily withhold their monsters and thus do not heavily rely on the scenario of physical threat. Julian Hanich places the first type of film at one edge of the horror spectrum, as these are primarily concerned with producing what he calls direct horror: "[they] repeatedly jolt the viewer out of the filmic world and draw him or her back into theatrical space" (*Cinematic Emotion* 253). The other end of the spectrum is occupied by films which mainly evoke emotions of "dread, terror and suggested horror" (253) and thus require a more cognitive-evaluative manner of viewing. This affective distinction is important to note, as it will lead to the main argument of this article, namely that an epistemological differentiation within Reyes' threat-theory needs to be conceived in order to accommodate films that are designed to evoke dread. That is to say, while threat still "lies at the heart of [every] horror experience" (104), the knowledge a horror film produces about a particular threat determines the way in which a viewer affectively experiences fear, ranging from extremely direct to extremely suggestive.

It may seem contradictory to suggest an affective-corporeal model of viewership, well suited to examine direct forms of horror, when taking a closer look at the emotion of dread, but it is important to keep some notions in mind. First off, the paradigm shift instigated by this theoretical model is essential for redefining horror. It separates the genre from Carroll's unnecessarily narrow theory and takes the affective experience of the genre center stage. "The experience of fear is multifaceted" (Hanfling 359) and therefore requires an in-depth phenomenological discussion. A second concern raised by Reyes is the genre's corporeal identity, which puts forward "the spectacle of a body caught in the grip of intense sensation or emotion" (L. Williams 4). This corporeal dimension is not only present on the level of representation, but also on the level of (pre)cognitive spectatorship: "the cinematic experience is also a sensory journey that extends beyond cognition (and the emotional affects this can bring about) and which can affect the audience physically" (Ndalianis 8-16). Feeling startled, anxious, disgusted: these are all typical reactions that horror films try to elicit with their viewers, some more successfully than others. In other words, horror films are not only perceived visually and aurally, but also haptically through a range of stimuli instigated by images and sounds.

From Leatherface to Cthulhu: Dread on the Spectrum

Where do we place dread as an emotion within this model? Reyes largely adopts Julian Hanich's ideas on the emotion, paying not much further attention since dread is not considered a crucial emotion in films that are focused on primarily producing direct horror. We shift the focus therefore to Hanich's work. In relation to cinema, Hanich speaks of the following: "the paradigm case of dread presents a vulnerable character who slowly and silently enters a dark, desolate place that harbors threat" (*Cinematic Emotion* 156). Such a terrifying scene implies an approaching confrontation, the outcome of which is always at least partially unknown. Hanich continues by distinguishing two main components in cinematic dread, i.e., (1) a form of fear in which the viewer empathizes with the threatened characters and (2) a secondary form of fear implying that the impending confrontation will be shocking and horrifying to witness (*Cinematic Emotion* 156). In other words, dread is a meta-emotion, i.e., an emotion that has other emotions (namely shock and horror) as its intentional object ("Judge Dread" 30). Emotions of shock and horror are generally the expected affective outcome of a typical dread-scene.

Fundamental to the emotion of dread is thus its anticipative nature, whereby tension is caused by the unknown (and potentially scary) outcome of an ongoing story and its (un)predictable patterns. In phenomenological terms, the lived experience of dread reflects a split intentionality. Building on the work of phenomenologist Herman Schmitz, Hanich makes a case for the distinction between that which the viewer is afraid of and the object that is its avatar (*Cinematic Emotion* 157). For example, when thinking about taking an exam, students do not consider the exam itself to be threatening, but rather the unpleasant consequences should they fail. In the case of cinematic dread, Hanich argues that the intentional object is far less coherent and therefore more elusive. A split occurs: on the one hand, the viewer fears for the characters who could be attacked and/or killed at any given moment; on the other hand, the viewer fears the confrontation itself, which usually results in emotions of shock and/or horror (*Cinematic Emotion* 157-158). The focus on distant temporality is therefore what distinguishes the emotion of dread from other fearful emotions such as shock, disgust or terror, which are largely focused on the immediate perception and proximity of the threatening object.

This cognitive-phenomenological approach conceptualizes dread as a preceding meta-emotion, with the main goal of generating fearful tension about something monstrous which remains (at least partially) veiled in a cloud of mystery. "Dread always requires a source of threat; no film can create a sense of dread without one" (116), writes Reyes. How well-defined a threat actually is, however, differs from film to film. Thus, building upon Reyes's threat theory, I opt to recognize dread in all forms of horror (from extremely direct to extremely suggestive) and not simply as an anticipatory emotion of a well-defined threat. In doing so, I attempt to reposition the emotion of dread to the center of the cinematic horror experience.

Readjusting that position becomes conceivable when situating the emotion of dread on Hanich's horror spectrum. On one end of the spectrum, we discover direct horror like Tobe Hooper's *The Texas Chainsaw Massacre*. With the (confirmed) presence of a chainsaw-wielding psychopath in the picture, dread is present, albeit to a lesser extent. During the course of the film, a viewer becomes fairly quickly aware of the lurking threat that is Leatherface, thus altering dread into horror and/or shock. This is not to say that, from the moment Leatherface is shown early-on in the story, there is no trace of dread within the film from there on. It is the case, however, that a film like *The Texas Chainsaw Massacre* is more interested in creatively evoking emotions of direct horror such as shock and disgust than dread. At the other end of the spectrum lies the evocative, unnamable horror like David R. Mitchell's *It Follows*, with "it" being an undefined threat that can take any possible shape or form. Here, fear transcends the known and rational, as "we never know if the danger might not potentially exceed our physic means of self-protection" (Hanich, *Cinematic Emotion* 159) and dread settles in more strongly, since the threat remains largely unknown throughout the entire course of the film.

Dread thus exists on the spectrum to which all horror films belong, although its intensity changes drastically from one end to the other. In other words, the emotion of dread is *inherent* to the cinematic horror experience, as its presence is felt in both direct horror films and suggestive horror films, albeit to very different extents based on epistemological variations. As such, the emotion of dread becomes elemental to the affective workings of cinematic horror. Considering the case studies Reyes mentions, which mainly exist within the scope of mutilation films, it should be stated that the threats in these types of horror films are tightly defined. Therefore, although dread-scenes are nonetheless present, they are structured around threats that are almost always (at least partially) revealed to viewers. It follows that the magnitude by which dread is felt during those scenes is limited, as viewers have a strong mental conceptualization of what to expect when the upcoming confrontation finally occurs. At the other end of the spectrum, however, are horror films that often explicitly withhold their threat from viewers and thus rely on establishing a sense of dread by consciously depriving viewers of their visibility to witness the suggested threat (Hanich, *Cinematic Emotion* 162).

In Horror Studies, such films are often associated with some form of Lovecraftian horror, which makes extensive use of dread-scenes. As mentioned above, Noël Carroll was the first to conceptualize the link between the Lovecraftian weird and the emotion of dread. Building on Lovecraft's own theory in *Supernatural Horror in Literature*, Brian Hauser even coins the term "weird cinema", which consists of three components: "the supernatural, an atmosphere of profound dread, and a seriousness of tone" (244). According to Hauser, weird cinema (e.g., Weir's *Picnic at Hanging Rock*, Wise's *The Haunting*, Parker's *Angel Heart*) implies that the suggested threat does not exist in the cinematic world, but rather haunts the imagination of characters and viewers alike. Consequently, the emotion of dread is heavily present in weird cinema, since it never fully acknowledges or confirms the threat's existence and allows for dread to settle in strongly. In similar vein, Cynthia Freeland associates dread, which she defines as "an anticipated encounter with something 'profound' - something particularly powerful" ("Horror and Art-Dread" 192), with a type of horror film that she terms "uncanny, where evil is a disembodied vague state of cosmic affairs" (*Naked and Undead* 215). To Freeland, uncanny horror explores the inconceivable horrors lying behind the barrier of human understanding and often taps into dread as an anticipative emotion to do so.

Dread-full films

The emotion of dread enjoys a prominent place in suggestive horror, whether it is termed "weird cinema" (Hauser) or "uncanny cinema" (Freeland). Yet these studies, despite their importance, tend to focus on connecting dread to ontological concepts such as Freud's uncanny or Lovecraft's cosmic weird and, in doing so, lose sight of the cognitive-phenomenological workings by which the emotion of dread structures the cinematic horror experience. In order, then, to show how the emotion of dread plays a pivotal role in structuring our affective experience of horror, the following segment will analyze two films that make use of dread most fully: Trey Edward Schults's *It Comes at Night* (2017) and Osgood Perkins's *The Blackcoat's Daughter* (alternative title: *February*) (2015).

The close readings below are based on the cognitive-phenomenological approach as discussed above. In particular, we take a closer look at the emotion of dread and its affective function within the selected films and report on both narrative and aesthetic elements that are significant in eliciting this emotion. On the one hand, the cognitive-focused reading examines the potential cues the film-text makes available in order to elicit dread. On the other hand, phenomenological-focused reading describes the corporeal viewing experience related to the emotional appraisal of dread. However, as indicated, Reyes develops his affective-corporeal model in relation to an apparent threat—something that is not present in the films below. Nevertheless, the close readings that follow showcase that dread-full films can also exist as part of Reyes's threat model and illustrate how the emotion of dread plays a major role in their affective experience. In fact, such films often use dread without being obliged to end up in shock and/or horror, but rather keep on echoing in the affective viewing experience, lingering on long after the film has ended.

Nuclear family in *It Comes at Night*

The cultural representation of "the nuclear family" has always been present throughout the history of the horror genre: from the monster-as-unwanted-child in Whale's *Frankenstein* (1931) through the monster-as-archaic-mother in Hitchcock's *Psycho* (1960) to familial disintegration in post-Vietnam slashers such as Craven's *The Hills Have Eyes* (1977). In horror, the heterosexual familial unit is often seen as inherently flawed and, subsequently, possesses the capacity to create monstrous beings (T. Williams). Schults's post-apocalyptic horror film *It Comes at Night* portrays such an archetypal family, where the source of evil is not some outside entity, but systematically destroys its members from within. To survive within this ever-changing society, the film seems to suggest, the nuclear family as a foundational structure is no longer a viable form of survival. In other words, as Kimberly Jackson puts it, such representations do "not imply that we have gotten beyond patriarchy but rather that it is no longer a functional model for describing social relations, yet it is so deeply entrenched we cannot envision an alternative" (*Gender and the Nuclear Family* 1).

It Comes at Night tells the story of a small family – father Paul (Joel Edgerton), mother Sarah (Carmen Ejogo), and son Travis (Kelvin Harrison) – who take refuge in their remote home deep in the woods after the outbreak of a contagious, undefined pandemic. The film starts off with the death of Grandfather Bud, who unfortunately has contracted and succumbed to the disease. Following his funeral, an unknown intruder breaks into the family's home, yet Paul manages to overpower him. When it becomes evident that the intruder, named Will

(Christopher Abbott), also has a wife (Riley Keough) and child (Griffin Faulkner) in dire need of help, Paul decides to take the family in. Both fathers seem to realize that they need each other's aid to increase their chance of survival.

It Comes at Night is the epitome of a dread-full film. What Hanich calls "narrative forewarning" (*Cinematic Emotion* 162) is omnipresent throughout. For example, viewers quickly learn that, based on the death of Grandfather Bud, the undefined disease that ravages the world is highly contagious and deadly. This feeling of danger is reinforced by the fact that the protagonists live in total isolation and each member of the family carries a gas mask and a rifle every time they go for a walk in the woods. In turn, the title of the film is fraught with a threatening undertone. As Bordwell, Staiger and Thompson note, "the most common sort of intertextual motivation is generic" (*Classical Hollywood Cinema* 18): references to other post-apocalyptic films automatically conjure up images of mutated, flesh-eating zombies. As a result of such deliberate techniques, the emotion of dread slowly builds up throughout the course of the film. A good example of this narrative build-up is a pivotal scene where Paul, Will and Travis are working outside near their house. Stanley, the family dog, suddenly starts barking out of nowhere. The scene continues with some reaction shots of Paul, Will and Travis, all while holding back from showing what Stanley is barking at. Hanich regards this editing technique as "a deliberate disregard of visibility" (163) whereby the film "refrain[s] from matching the eyeline – or at least protract[s] it deliberately" (166). This lack of visibility elicits dread, since the film acknowledges that there is a lurking threat out there but prevents viewers from visualizing anything. When the scene finally cuts to

Stanley's perspective, only the image of a boundless forest is shown. As an "endless space" (*Cinematic Emotion* 175), the forest harbors many dangers without any form of protection for the threatened characters. Throughout its course, *It Comes at Night* suggestively establishes a life-threatening danger in its post-apocalyptic world but reveals practically nothing about it: "our epistemic deficit in dread scenes creates an expectation of the worst: the unknown, potentially enormous horror that might await us at the end of the scene is particularly terrifying because the threat is not only hinted at but not clearly spelled out" (*Cinematic Emotion* 159). Schults's film is a prime example of this.

When Stanley eventually runs into the woods, Travis decides to follow him. The film suddenly cuts to a wide shot of Travis, who seems to be all alone in this great wilderness, "enwrapped, as it were, by its frightening spell" (Hanich, *Cinematic Emotion* 176). Travis keeps on running until Stanley's barking dies out. A deadly silence – both in image and sound – falls over the scene as Travis, his gun quivering in front of him, stares anxiously into the distance. The image once again cuts to an eye-line match of the endless forest, inviting viewers to scour the horizon in search of any possible threat. Once again, the image reveals nothing. Soon after, Paul and Will come to the rescue and the three of them return home, leaving Stanley behind.

That same night, a sleepless Travis roams inside the house and discovers Andrew, Will's son, sleeping on the living room floor. Travis wakes him up and leads Andrew back to his room. While returning to his own room, Travis suddenly hears a thumping noise inside the house and decides to explore. As mentioned before, "the paradigm case of dread presents a vulnerable character slowly and quietly entering a dark, forsaken place harboring threat" (Hanich, *Cinematic Emotion* 156), which is exactly what Shults presents here. An oppressive atmosphere pervades the entire scene. Throughout its course, viewers do not gain any insight into the architecture of the rooms in which Travis wanders about. Similar to the Overlook Hotel in Kubrick's *The Shining*, the house is presented as a complex labyrinth that evokes an uneasy feeling of danger lurking behind every corner of every room. While searching for the source of the strange sound, the only light source present in the entire scene is the lamp that Travis is holding in his hands, resulting in an almost all-encompassing darkness, once again preventing viewers from visualizing the spaces in which Travis resides.

A second cue that is used in this scene is what Hanich calls the rejection of "the principle of temporal economy" (167). In other words, the scene takes a relatively long time compared to others. This "slowing-down" is essential to the overall atmosphere of a dread-full experience. Despite the long duration, such scenes are "quite the opposite of boring. Since our lived-bodies are affected directly, the anticipation of shock or horror rivets us even tighter to the screen" (Hanich, *Cinematic Emotion* 169). This is exemplified in *It Comes at Night* by the accentuation of Travis's every move throughout the house, visualized by wide shots of him walking in different rooms. Such sequences arouse suspicion, as viewers become glued to the screen waiting for something to happen. When Travis finally arrives at the entrance of the house - the source of the unfamiliar sound being very near him - the film slows down even more. A ping-pong montage ensues between Travis and the red door at the end of the long entrance hall. Any moment now, the scene can turn into a shocking and horrifying moment, and the emotion of dread reaches its peak in terms of intensity. A loud banging noise abruptly breaks the silence, after which dread turns into shock: "at the speed of light and sound, the film pushes forward, forces on and closes in on the viewer who literally retreats, resiles, recoils in a very real sense" (Hanich, *Cinematic Emotion* 146).

After Travis wakes up the others, Paul and Will discover that the noise came from Stanley, who somehow managed to get into the house but turns out to be infected. It soon becomes clear that Andrew has also fallen ill. The virus quickly spreads amongst all family members and, after an intense confrontation, Paul's wife decides to kill Will as he is probably infected too. Paul, in turn, shoots Kim and Andrew. But the damage is done as Travis turns out to be infected as well. The film ends on a dramatic note with a wide shot of Paul and Sarah sitting across each other at the dinner table, all alone as everyone else has died. *It Comes at Night* paints a dark portrait of intrafamilial decay. No flesh-eating zombies are at the root of this tragedy, but families seem to have the capacity to destroy each other from within. What comes at night is not a physical threat from outside, but the prevailing sense of paranoia and mistrust amongst people in times of crisis. It is the obscure force of human instinct, when civil structures cave in, that drives both families to their own demise. Even with all the pragmatic constructions that Paul sets up to keep his family safe, there is no escaping the primal nature of humanity that manifests itself when the struggle for survival takes over.

The affective experience of *It Comes at Night* is fundamentally tied to the emotion of dread, which is arguably present from the first until the last shot of this film. Besides the dread-scenes mentioned above, *It Comes at Night* manages to establish a "physical" threat that remains elusive at best yet nonetheless pervades the entire film. Even at the end, viewers have practically no knowledge of the deadly virus but are frightfully aware of its destructive capacities. As such, the emotion of dread affectively guides the cinematic horror experience of *It Comes at Night* and in doing so, becomes essential to the film's emotional resonance with viewers.

Demonic religion in *The Blackcoat's Daughter*

The Blackcoat's Daughter, directed by Osgood Perkins, was released in 2015. The film's story starts when Rose (Lucy Boynton) and Kat (Kiernan Shipka) are left behind at the start of a one-week holiday in February and both girls are required to stay at their Catholic boarding school. There, Kat falls under the spell of the Devil, whose presence is suggested but never seen, and orders her to kill Rose and two remaining nuns. The plot itself is divided into three different timelines, each named after one of the main characters. In doing so, the film actively engages its viewers, who are required to assemble the story according to the evolving plot, revealing more and more information about Kat and her demonic possession along the way. As a result, anticipation of something monstrous seeps into the minds of viewers without ever manifesting itself. Dread thus becomes a crucial emotion in the film's cinematic experience.

The first dread-scene occurs when Rose returns from her secret date. On the toilet in the dorm's restroom, she suddenly hears a girl's voice, resembling Kat's, through the radiator's pipes. Rose decides to retrace the origin of the strange sound, a decision that leads her to the basement of the building. The film uses this claustrophobic space to elicit dread. Building on Bachelard's concept of intimate spaces, Hanich states that "we descend into the depths of the cellar on stairs leading down ... removed from the world outside [it] manages to further enhance our feelings of constriction and isolation" (174). In *The Blackcoat's Daughter*, the basement is shrouded in darkness, which—combined with a tight framing on Rose's face—feels extremely confined to viewers. The source of the strange-sounding voice is a small room on the other side. As Rose slowly walks towards it, the film emphasizes her every step through its paced editing. Here, too, narrative economy is rejected to create tension and a feeling of distrust with viewers. Once she has arrived, Rose glances through the window of the small door. Instead of an expected eye-line match, the film shows her shocked reaction, only to cut to the sight that shocked her a few seconds later: Kat kneeling in front of a heating boiler while passionately praying to an unknown entity.

Gradually, both viewers and Rose realize that there is something fundamentally wrong with Kat. When Kat aggressively lashes out at the two nuns the next afternoon, Rose is sent off to clear some snow off the sidewalk. At this point in the film, Kat's timeline is introduced. Viewers discover that Kat has been in contact with a malicious entity, the Devil, for several days now. Kat kills and beheads both nuns. The film cuts back to Rose, who is lying down on her bed. When she wakes up to go to the toilet, she suddenly hears a door slam shut. Someone, most likely Kat, is near her. Dread creeps into the viewing experience, this time stronger than before due to a viewer's newly obtained knowledge: Kat is evil and capable of murder.

What follows is an archetypal example of the "alone-in-the-dark" scenario. Rose walks out of the bathroom, calling out Kat's name repeatedly. She does not know, however, what Kat is capable of and her fear is therefore more groundless compared to the one viewers experience simultaneously. What frightens viewers is the fate of Rose (for whom they feel empathy), but mainly their own fate, as the scene can turn into a shocking and/or terrifying moment at any point. Implicit cues in the scene's cinematography, editing and soundscape point to something ominous that is about to be revealed: long corridors showing nothing but darkness, tight framing suggesting a large off-screen space, and an unnerving silence in the sound design.

When Rose finally arrives at the end of the stairwell, she makes a terrifying discovery that is partially withheld. Rose looks towards the ground and an eye-line match follows her searching gaze. However, before a viewer can see the terrifying object that Rose is confronted with, the film cuts back to a close-up of Rose, who looks distressed. A second eye-line match shows a pool of blood with some dirty rags lying next to the stairs. The film quickly cuts to Rose, who walks away in utter shock, back into the hallway. Suddenly, Kat appears from around the corner, accompanied by the sound of shrilling violins. She stabs Rose several times before Rose falls to the ground and dies. Such an intense sequence is the prototypical outcome of a nerve-racking dread scene: "a short, highly compressed form of fear. It responds to a threatening object or event that suddenly and unexpectedly opens up the situation" (Hanich 127). Strongly linked to all kinds of aesthetic trickeries, this intense moment is of an overall corporeal nature: viewers jump out of their seats, turn their heads away, cry out in shock. Film-techniques such as abrupt cuts, the intrusion of off-screen elements into an on-screen space, and the active presence of loud music often exploit this direct link between fast-paced moving images and viewers' embodied viewing experience (Hanich, *Cinematic Emotion* 133-138).

Once the authorities discover Kat's heinous crime, she is quickly apprehended. The school's minister decides to perform an exorcism on Kat. The Devil leaves her body, although Kat, having grown quite fond of her weird companion, does not want the Devil to leave. Following this scene, the film's third timeline—named after Joan (Emma Roberts), the third protagonist in the film—is introduced to viewers. Viewers quickly learn that Joan is an older Kat. After escaping from a mental institution, Joan/Kat murders and beheads three people once again. She then travels to the scene of the original crime in an attempt to summon the Devil she lost years ago. But only silence and solitude meet her. All alone and abandoned, Kat leaves the boarding school and collapses in the middle of the road.

Horror and religion share an intertwined and complex history (Beal and Greenaway, *Horror and Religion*), mainly due to the many religious themes that the genre frequently exploits: sin and redemption, life after death, the struggle between good and evil, and the presence of the supernatural (Stone). The role of the Catholic Church as last-minute lifesaver is a well known trope in horror. One simply needs to think of films such as Friedkin's *The Exorcist* or Wan's *The Conjuring*, which consistently use Christian faith as a weapon against (but also source of) evil. However, in an ostensibly secularized world, *The Blackcoat's Daughter* shows a more pessimistic portrayal of these institutions. The Devil seems to hide in places where we do not expect Him, even next to heating boilers in abandoned basements of Catholic institutions or in the minds of faithful schoolgirls who feel lonely and vulnerable.

Similar to *It Comes at Night*, *The Blackcoat's Daughter* succeeds in establishing an affective experience that is primarily guided by the emotion of dread. As an omnipresent entity, the Devil lurks behind protagonist Kat like a shadowy figure, following her every move. While viewers are made aware that this entity poses a dangerous threat, its presence remains vague and ambiguous at best. However, the film succeeds in leaving breadcrumbs throughout its course, allowing viewers to become frightened of an impending confrontation. As such, dread is present throughout the entire film, meticulously built up around pivotal scenes such as the ones described above.

Conclusion

As mentioned, dread exists as an anticipatory emotion that mainly focuses on a prospective confrontation with the monstrous. What exactly that monstrous entails is always (at least partially) unknown. One simply needs to consider the films mentioned above: an unknown virus or demonic possession, these are threats with which a horror viewer is familiar. Nevertheless, these films shed new light on such entities, mainly through the creative use of dread. According to the cognitive-phenomenological approach outlined above, dread results in moments of shock and/or horror, which resolve the mystery surrounding the monster and therefore eliminate dread. But these dreadfull films never reveal everything, leaving viewers in a perpetual state of uncertainty and eliciting dread as a "lingering" emotion. *It Comes at Night* elicits dread without ever revealing the infectious disease that is omnipresent throughout the film. In similar vein, *The Blackcoat's Daughter* manages to evoke a dreadful experience of demonic possession without defining any concrete threat. In the end, these films pose more questions than they answer and in doing so, aim to generate a discourse demanding contemplation of what is being shown. The monstrous manifestations in these films do not necessarily represent the monstrous real but have a symbolic value that pertains to obscure forces (cf. mutating nature in *It Comes at Night* and dangerous religion in *The Blackcoat's Daughter*). What guides the affective experience of these films is the way in which the emotion of dread is constructed throughout their course. By means of a cognitive-phenomenological reading this study has aimed to showcase that, in these films, dread is not simply anticipative in nature, but inherently structures and guides the overall cinematic horror experience. In doing so, it becomes an intrinsic emotion that should take center stage in future theorization of cinematic affect in Horror Studies. As long as the veil of mystery lingers on, dread will reverberate in the spectatorship of these films.

Notes

1. Spectatorship is a heavily contested term within Film Studies and its history goes as far back as the academic discipline itself. This article builds upon cognitive and phenomenological film theory, which state that (a) spectators play an active role in constructing the unity of a film, both cognitively and emotionally (cf. cognitive film theory), and that (b) the bodily viewing experience has to be accounted for in film-analysis (cf. film-phenomenology).

2. When talking about "the viewer", I consider this term from within the film-text itself, in accordance with the theoretical frameworks of cognitive film theory and film-phenomenology. In other words, "the viewer" is purely hypothetical and conceptual in nature, and hence transhistorical and transcultural. Every reference to this term or word throughout the text refers to this theoretical understanding of viewership. Such a universalist approach, however, may seem problematic to some. While it would take more than a full-length paper to delve into these matters, I do wish to clarify some important concerns. It is important to bear in mind that, while the article discusses the affective relationship between moving images and spectators, any conclusion drawn from a purely textual inquiry is considered an intended or preferred reading. Nothing, then, can and will be said about the actual readings of actual audiences. In my opinion, this does not imply that universalist approaches are by definition unreliable, since both cognitive film theory and film-phenomenology are highly developed research strands based on empirically grounded and methodologically rigorous research, on which this study is based. This, however, is not to dismiss the validity and contribution of audience studies, as I believe both text-based and audience-based research can coexist alongside each other.

Works Cited

Angel Heart. Directed by Alan Parker, Carolco Pictures and Tri-Star Pictures, 1987.

Bachelard, Gaston. *The Poetics of Space*. 1958. Beacon Press, 1994.

Beal, Eleanor, and Jonathan Greenaway, editors. *Horror and Religion: New Literary Approaches to Theology, Race and Sexuality*. University of Wales Press, 2019.

Bordwell, David. "Cognitive Theory." *The Routledge Companion to Philosophy and Film*, edited by Paisley Livingston and Carl Plantinga, Routledge, 2009, pp. 357 – 367.

---. *Narration in the Fiction Film*. University of Wisconsin Press, 1985.
Bordwell, David, and Staiger, Janet, and Thompson, Kristin. *The Classical Hollywood Cinema: Film Style and Mode of Production to 1960*. 1985. Routledge, 1988.
Carroll, Noël. *The Philosophy of Horror: or, Paradoxes of The Heart*. Routledge, 1990.
Frankenstein. Directed by James Whale, Universal Pictures, 1931.
Freeland, Cynthia. A. *The Naked and the Undead: Evil and the Appeal of Horror*. Westview Press, 2000.
---. "Horror and Art-Dread". *The Horror Film*, edited by Stephen Prince, Rutgers University Press, 2004, pp. 189 – 205.
Gregg, Melissa, and Gregory J. Seigworth, editors. *The Affect Theory Reader*. Duke University Press, 2010.
Grodal, Torben. *Moving Pictures: A New Theory of Film Genres, Feelings, and Cognition*. Oxford University Press, 1999.
Hanfling, Oswald. "Fact, Fiction and Feeling." *The British Journal of Aesthetics*, vol. 36, no. 4, 1996, pp. 356 – 366.
Hanich, Julian. *Cinematic Emotion in Horror Films and Thrillers: The Aesthetic Paradox of Pleasurable Fear*, Routledge, 2011.
---. "Judge Dread: What We Are Afraid of When We Are Scared of Movies." *Projections*, vol. 8, no. 2, pp. 26 – 49.
Hauser, Brian. R. "Weird Cinema and the Aesthetics of Dread." *New Directions in Supernatural Horror Literature: The Critical Influence of H.P. Lovecraft*, edited by Sean Moreland, Palgrave Macmillan, 2018, pp. 235 – 252.
Hills, Matt. "An Event-Based Definition of Art-Horror." *Dark Thoughts: Philosophic Reflections on Cinematic Horror*, edited by Steven Jay Schneider and Daniel Shaw, Scarecrow Press, 2003, pp. 138 - 157.
Husserl, Edmund. *Ideas: General Introduction to Pure Phenomenology*. 1931. Routledge, 2012.

It Comes at Night. Directed by Trey Edward Schults, Animal Kingdom and A24, 2017.

It Follows. Directed by David R. Mitchell, Northern Lights Films et al., 2014.

Jackson, Kimberly. *Gender and the Nuclear Family in Twenty-First-Century Horror*. Palgrave Macmillan, 2015.

Leeder, Murray. "David Robert Mitchell's *It Follows* (2014)." *Horror: A Companion*, edited by Simon Bacon, Peter Lang Publishing, 2016, pp. 11 – 17.

Lovecraft, Howard P. *Supernatural Horror in Literature & Other Literary Essays*. 1927. Wildside Press, 2011.

Merleau-Ponty, Maurice. *Phenomenology of Perception*. 1962. Routledge, 2002.

Ndalianis, Angela. *The Horror Sensorium: Media and the Senses*. McFarland & Company, 2012.

Picnic at Hanging Rock. Directed by Peter Weir, British Empire Films et al., 1975

Plantinga, Carl. "Emotion and Affect." *The Routledge Companion to Philosophy and Film*, edited by Paisley Livingston and Carl Plantinga, Routledge, 2009, pp. 86 – 96.

Pyscho. Directed by Alfred Hitchcock, Shamley Productions, 1960.

Reyes, Xavier. A. *Horror Film and Affect: Towards A Corporeal Model of Viewership*. Routledge, 2018.

Saw. Directed by James Wan, Twisted Pictures, 2004.

Scarry, Elaine. *The Body in Pain: The Making and Unmaking of the World*. Oxford University Press, 1985.

Schmitz, Hermann. *Der Gefühlsraum*. Bouvier, 1969

Smith, Murray. *Engaging Characters: Fiction, Emotion, and the Cinema*. Oxford University Press, 1995.

Smuts, Aaron. "Horror." *The Routledge Companion to Philosophy and Film*, edited by Paisley Livingston and Carl Plantinga, Routledge, 2009, pp. 505 – 514.

Sobchack, Vivian. "Phenomenology." *The Routledge Companion to Philosophy and Film*, edited by Paisley

Livingston and Carl Plantinga, Routledge, 2009, pp. 435 – 445.

Stone, Bryan. "The Sanctification of Fear: Images of the Religious in Horror Films." *Journal of Religion & Film*, vol. 5, no. 2, pp. 1 – 32, 2001.

Tan, Ed. S. *Emotion and the structure of narrative film: film as an emotion machine*. Erlbaum, 1996.

Texas Chainsaw Massacre. Directed by Tobe Hooper, Vortex, 1974.

The Blackcoat's Daughter. Directed by Osgood Perkins, Paris Film et al., 2015.

The Conjuring. Directed by James Wan, New Line Cinema et al., 2013.

The Exorcist. Directed by William Friedkin, Warner Bros. Pictures and Hoya Productions, 1973.

The Haunting. Directed by Robert Wise, Argyle Enterprises, 1963.

The Hills Have Eyes. Directed by Wes Craven, Blood Relations Company, 1977.

The Shining. Directed by Stanley Kubrick, Warner Bros. et al., 1980.

Thompson, Kirsten. M. *Apocalyptic Dread: American Film at the Turn of the Millennium*. State University of New York Press, 2007.

Williams, Linda. "Film Bodies: Gender, Genre, and Excess." *Film Quarterly*, vol. 44, no. 4, 1991, pp. 2 – 13.

Williams, Tony. *Hearths of Darkness: The Family in the American Horror Film, Updated Edition*. University Press of Mississippi, 2015.

Zahavi, Dan. *Phenomenology: The Basics*. Routledge, 2019.

[•REC]. Directed by Jaume Balagueró and Paco Plaza, Filmax International and Castelao Productions, 2007.

Atomic Art and the Ecological Perspectives of David Lynch

Todd Tietchen

ATOMIC ART HAS MUCH TO TELL US about our precarious existence in the Anthropocene. As a designation, Atomic Art accounts for creative work responding to the events and potentially devastating hazards of the nuclear age, including nuclear detonations, nuclear warfare, nuclear proliferation, radionuclide fallout, and nuclear waste. Recent critical works such as Gabrielle Decamous's *Invisible Colors: The Arts of the Atomic Age* (MIT 2018) and Rosemary A. Joyce's *The Future of Nuclear Waste: What Art and Archeology Can Tell Us about Securing the World's Most Hazardous Material* (Oxford 2020) have done much to deepen our appreciation of the characteristics of Atomic Art. One of the persistent qualities of the wide array of atomic artworks discussed by Decamous and Joyce is their unambiguous treatment of the escalating fragility of human and other life-worlds in our post-Hiroshima times, a quality that makes Atomic Art an exemplary aesthetic tradition of the

Anthropocene. Tellingly, Atomic Art's focus on the precarity of our lives and ecosystems is a quality also found in much of our recent scholarship, literature, and art addressing anthropogenic climate crisis. Indeed, those of us troubled about environmental destruction and our imperiled planetary future should take the concerns of Atomic Art just as seriously as we take the devastation of wetlands, forests, food webs, and other ecological systems, for they serve equally as signposts of our vulnerability.

Along with the scholarly work of Decamous and Joyce, the filmic and televisual work of David Lynch might assist us in more clearly understanding this connection between Atomic Art and ecological crisis. As it turns out, Lynch's work has always represented an essential engagement with the Anthropocene and its aesthetic forms, an engagement which compellingly connects the advent of the atomic age and the acceleration of ecological crisis. Episode 8 of *Twin Peaks: The Return*, "Gotta Light?" makes this connection explicitly, linking planetary and ecological crisis to the advent of the nuclear age in ways that broaden our understanding of Lynch's ecological perspectives more generally. Writing of episode 8 on the Twin Peaks fan site 25YL, Lindsay Stamhuis observes that Lynch had decisively placed the July 1945 Trinity detonation, which features prominently in the episode, "at the very heart of [Twin Peaks'] myth-building exercise," remarking that its inclusion "has suddenly imbued Twin Peaks with a sense of depth that is, at its core, rooted deeply in the fabric of our history." On its own, Lynch's detonation sequence is an astounding and disconcerting addition to Atomic Art, though, as Stamhuis suggests, episode 8 simultaneously asks us to revisit our assumptions regarding the series' cosmological foundations or the historical implications of its "myth-building exercise." In the nearly three decades since *Twin Peaks* first premiered on ABC in 1990, environmental devastation and its many repercussions have continued to accelerate, and "Gotta Light?" frames the historical dawning of the Anthropocene in an appropriately tragic and frightening light.[1]

Twin Peaks: The Return premiered on Showtime in 2017 and is the third season of Lynch's influential television series. In what follows, I hope to suggest that the concerns of its eighth episode shed some timely light on the broader ecological ramifications of Lynch's work in *Twin Peaks* and elsewhere, while allowing for an equally pertinent discussion of other influential works of Atomic Art that "Gotta Light?" so clearly references. Through the episode's allusive density, Lynch helps bring the canon of Atomic Art into focus while foregrounding some of its signature characteristics and trepidations. Those trepidations include the genesis and acceleration of the Anthropocene, the continued legacies of androcentrism, the desecration of Indigenous landscapes and cosmologies, and the increased saliency of post-nature perspectives for viewing the legacies of environmental destruction and ecological disregard in our post-Hiroshima times.

Depicting the Nuclear Anthropocene

At the center of "Gotta Light?" is a surreal depiction of the July 1945 Trinity event in which "the Gadget," an implosion-design plutonium device, was detonated in New Mexico's Jornado del Muerto desert. This sequence begins at the episode's 16:20 mark. We are initially shown the Trinity blast from a great distance (an extreme long shot), and Lynch suspends the duration of the detonation long enough to track into its mushroom cloud slowly, plunging us into the murky, interminable quantum fog that somehow fashions our concrete, perceivable universe. Accompanied by Krzysztof Penderecki's *Threnody to the Victims of Hiroshima*, Lynch ushers us into swirling vacillations of light and dark, then something closely resembling television static, then a black void in which atomic particles fall and swirl, and finally clouds illumined by interstellar light that form into a vortex. The vortex forming in Lynch's impressionistic atomic cloud is in fact a portal for negative or malevolent extradimensional entities, the chief among them BOB, a manifestation of depraved and conscienceless male violence. BOB, years later, will possess Leland Palmer, the father of Laura Palmer, whose death at Leland-BOB's hands, after years of sexual assault, is the event that sets *Twin Peaks* in motion. For much of its initial two seasons, *Twin Peaks* is in part a murder-mystery focused upon the death of Laura, presented in an episodic format mirroring the nighttime soap operas (such as *Dallas* and *Falcon Crest*) that became so popular during the 1980s.

The Trinity detonation is BOB's origin story, rendered figuratively at the 24:00 mark at which point we witness the detonation vomiting BOB into the world, along with numerous eggs carrying hatchlings, which some viewers of the show have come to refer to as "frog-moths" on account of their mutated appearance upon leaving their shells over a decade later. At the 40:45 mark of "Gotta Light?" Lynch takes us back to the New Mexican desert on August 5, 1956, and during that sequence a character identified in the credits as The Woodsman wanders out of the desert onto the local highway and asks terrified travelers for a light for his cigarette. True to his name, The Woodsman wears lumberjack attire (including a checker-patterned flannel shirt) and his bearded face is deeply smeared with soot. Unsuccessful in his attempts to secure a light for his cigarette—as those he encounters flee in terror—he soon after commandeers the local radio station and uses the airwaves to incant: "This is the water, and this is the well. Drink full and descend. The horse is the white of the eyes, and dark within." The incantation is a soporific and allows, over the remaining course of this narrative sequence, for one of the newly hatched frog-moths (or hatchlings) to enter the body of a sleeping human host, a teenage New Mexican girl. The frog-moth—a mutated, winged frog—climbs into her mouth and is ingested, though the teenager's sleeping expression remains placid.

Currently, there are numerous timelines and theoretical perspectives competing to define the catalyzing events of the Anthropocene, and the New Mexican sequences from "Gotta Light?" mirror those models that situate the onset of the Anthropocene within the Atomic Age. In 2015, the scientific membership of the Anthropocene Working Group (AWP) identified the Trinity Test as the *golden spike* of the Anthropocene, though in May 2019 the AWP slightly adjusted its recommended start date to the mid-twentieth century more generally.[2] This revision was attributed to the marked profusion of radionuclides in planetary stratigraphy as a result of more frequent nuclear testing during the 1950s; prior to that, radioactive elements remained largely confined to local sites, producing mutated rocks like Trinitite, a glassy hybrid of desert sand and minerals that many have seen as tremendously important to dating the onset of the Anthropocene. But as Jeremy Davies points out, Trinitite's "geological impact did not extend beyond the [Trinity detonation] site itself," so that those looking to find a golden spike of radionuclide fallout in the geological record would be better served by the six years stretching from 1952 to 1958, during which time detonations "by the United States, Soviet Union, and United Kingdom in the tropical Pacific and Kazakhstan spread increasing volumes of radioactive fallout all around the world" (104). Included within that lamentable period was the Castle Bravo event, which featured the most powerful thermonuclear weapon ever detonated in the Pacific by the United States. Its detonation was three miles wide and killed everything for miles around, down to the ocean floor, constituting one of the most horrific singular acts of violence enacted by humans on the planet's oceans.

Lynch's dating of the sequence featuring the Woodsman and the hatchlings as August 5, 1956, falls within this period of intensified testing and environmental destruction, during which radionuclide fallout became more prevalent in planetary stratigraphy. Indeed, from May to July 1956, the United States carried out seventeen detonations in the South Pacific known as Operation Redwing, with each detonated weapon named for a Native American tribe. August 5 initiated the first new lunar cycle following Operation Redwing's conclusion—and the hatchlings are new births. They are also newly invasive radioactivity. Operation Redwing represents a particularly toxic period of U.S. nuclear activity, and upon its termination Lynch's frog-moths hatch and begin to migrate beyond their irradiated nests of sand. In a sense,

80 • Todd Tietchen

the atomic sequence at the heart of episode 8 acknowledges both golden spikes proffered by the AWP, the initial and revised.

As Gabrielle Decamous explains throughout *Invisible Colors*, nuclear aesthetics must inevitably deal with the conundrum of representing radioactivity, the presence of which is not detectable through human senses. In the case of "Gotta Light?" Lynch has chosen BOB and the mutated hatchlings to fulfill this representational task. Obviously, the mutant form of the hatchlings mirrors other atomic visions of the monstrous, the Japanese kaiju Godzilla being perhaps the quintessential example of the mutated creatures so prevalent within the Atomic Art of the 1950s and 1960s. This particular mutant—Lynch's frog-moth—can fly, for the aftereffects of detonations have wings (in a manner of speaking). Irradiation is incredibly difficult to contain. It travels—and in this case, the sleeping teenager becomes contaminated without her knowledge or permission, her physiology breached without her cognizance. Some devoted viewers of the show see the frog-moths as homing devices that identify their hosts as sites for possession by malevolent transdimensional entities in the future.[3] From that perspective, the frog-moths are cancerous in a sense; they represent radioactive pervasiveness gestating into something worse, festering into malignancies, and indeed that also describes Leland's habitation by BOB over a number of years, as BOB claims possession of Leland's physiology incrementally but decisively.

Fourteen minutes into Ishirō Honda's Anthropocene masterpiece, *Godzilla* (1954), the titular *kaiju* attacks a small village just as a typhoon hits, leaving his irradiated

81 • Todd Tietchen

footprints behind. Shortly thereafter, the zoologist Dr. Yamane informs us that "hydrogen-bomb testing has driven [Godzilla] from its natural habitat," much as the Trinity blast releases BOB in *Twin Peaks: The Return*. Indeed, as Decamous contends, "because the atomic age at large introduced new forms of lethal warfare as well as radioactive contamination, leaks, accidents, irradiation, and the need for evacuation zones, the art of the atomic age is first and foremost an art of catastrophe" (253), and we see that depicted in the Cold War aesthetic tradition of mutated monsters such as Godzilla, and in films such as *Them* (1954), *Attack of the Crab Monster* (1957), and *Behemoth: The Sea Monster* (1958). *Godzilla*, to which Lynch clearly alludes in "Gotta Light?" remains a seminal text in this representational tradition.

In the radioactive frog-moths we confront the dangerous, perhaps deadly, intimacies between human and nonhuman entities, between the human form and toxic vibrant matter characteristic of our post-Hiroshima lives. This element of Lynch's nuclear aesthetic also has numerous precursors in Cold War narratives of habitation and contamination, such as *Invaders from Mars* (1953), *The Gamma People* (1956), *Wasp Woman* (1959), *X: The Man with the X-Ray Eyes* (1963), and the human mutants worshipping the doomsday bomb in *Beneath the Planet of the Apes* (1970). Moreover, tales of nuclear apocalypse and habitation abound in 1950s science fiction and fantasy publications such as *The Magazine of Fantasy and Science Fiction*, *Imagination* (renamed *Imaginative Tales* in 1954) and *Satellite Science Fiction*, as the initial anxieties of the atomic age also helped foster the development of a robust tradition of Anthropocene print culture, an aesthetic

82 • Todd Tietchen

history nested in "Gotta Light?" alongside other influences from Cold War science fiction.

Timothy Morton's use of the descriptor "viscosity" to describe the toxic intimacies which trouble our notions of an inside/outside duality mediated by human physiology is particularly helpful for thinking about such narratives. There is something demonic in the viscous nature of radiation, in its propensity to become radically internal. Indeed, in his analysis of hyperobjects, Morton asserts that "the demonic Twin Peaks character Bob," capable of possessing and warping the human form, reveals the agential capacities of harmful entities that remain impenetrable to human observation (29). Morton counts "all of the nuclear materials on Earth" among such entities, identifying them collectively as a hyperobject. Morton defines hyperobjects as "things that are [so] massively distributed in time and space relative to humans," that they defy our abilities to discern and map them (1). Indeed, the planetary climate crisis is itself a hyperobject and may be gathered under Morton's schema, along with proliferate nuclear materials and radionuclides, within the hyperobject known as the Anthropocene. Put somewhat differently, the problem of depicting radionuclides is the problem of depicting our incrementally intensifying climate crisis, as the former is contained within the latter.

Gordon Cole, the Deputy Director of the FBI played in *Twin Peaks* by Lynch himself, encounters the issue of the hyperobject's resistance to representation at the 15:35 mark of return season episode 16, "No Knock, No Doorbell." In the short scene in question, Cole sits befuddled in a room crowded with humming computational technology, deeply troubled by his inability to resolve the transdimensional havoc being wreaked by BOB and Jowday, or "Judy," another of the malevolent entities populating Lynch's mythos. Cole's puzzlement results from the fact that all of his advanced computational technology has made him deeply aware of the fact that he cannot map the situation confronting him—that the entities and processes set free in his corner of the multiverse are somehow too excessive to their rendering, just as the hearing aid he wears throughout the series does not keep him from routinely mishearing people, often at critical moments.

Cole's conundrum is of course Lynch's own conundrum in terms of representing the nonsensuous properties of nuclear detonations and radioactivity. Lynch's aesthetic solution in *Twin Peaks* involves pulling from a wide range of sources, as he couples representational strategies found in genre works such as *Godzilla* with expressive practices originating in the Cold War avant-garde. Writing in *Slate* shortly after the airing of episode 8, Sam Adams described the portal created by the Trinity detonation as "a celestial birth canal" bearing BOB into the world, and pointed out the sequence's artistic debt to Stan Brakhage and Bruce Conner—though Adams does not elaborate beyond his passing observation. Conner's influence is particularly evident in Lynch's decision to extend the duration of the Trinity detonation so that he might track into it, thus revealing the entrance of BOB into our world. This sequence powerfully recalls elements of Bruce Conner's *Crossroads*, a 1976 assemblage film in which Conner uses slow-motion footage of the July 25, 1946, nuclear detonation at Bikini Atoll in the Pacific to construct a highly influential work of investigative cinema. The blast was filmed by over 500 cameras for research purposes, and Conner reassembles a selection of this archival footage—shot in slow-motion from multiple perspectives—into a study of the blast, images of which we are exposed to numerous times during the collage film's thirty-seven minutes. I refer to this as investigative cinema, for Conner asks the viewer to consider the blast from varying perspectives at extremely slow speeds to comprehend the enormity of what has occurred at this civilizational "crossroads." We might, however, read the film as commenting simultaneously on fallout and irradiation, which pose such significant representational challenges for atomic artworks. Ultimately, Conner shows us that these blasts are not contained within a solitary detonation event—or, to say it differently, the contents of the blast are not fully identical with the specter of the detonation. Over and over again we are exposed to the effects of nuclear detonations in the form of radionuclides; repeatedly our bodies and ecosystems experience the event.

During the Cold War era, the existential and environmental concerns raised by atomic science and nuclear weaponry seized the imagination of the avant-garde in a significant way.[4] *Crossroads* exemplifies this development, as does Stan Brakhage's *23rd Psalm Branch* (1967). Like *Crossroads* and much of Brakhage's oeuvre, *23rd Psalm Branch* is an assemblage film combining historical and reportorial footage with Brakhage's own non-narrative camera work and hand-painted frames. The film alternates notably in its source material between images of cataclysmic bombing, warfare, and death, including images of the holocaust and atomic mushroom clouds. This collage of disturbing images is interrupted

85 • Todd Tietchen

now and again with footage from a mobile camera racing through a nondescript landscape, propelling us forward without discernible narrative reason toward the next cycle of death, explosions, and atomic detonations. When Brakhage scratches the message "I can't go on" across the frames of one such progression, the "I" in question appears to be Western history itself—a continuum of semi-organized violence and technologically enhanced destruction advancing unstoppably toward a momentous doom made ever more tangible through the atomic weaponry used to end the Second World War. Brakhage's rapid editing reinforces the impression of pushing forward, of being driven in a captive fashion, unable to escape the terrible momentum of our new circumstances.[5] Like Conner, Brakhage also repeats the same cycles of imagery so that we seem propelled forward at the very same time that we are caught in a cycle, looping back continuously on our destructive tendencies. As in *Crossroads*, we live through the repercussions of these events perpetually. We cannot outrun what we have released.

Just as he absorbed the influence of Honda and tropes from Cold War science fiction, Lynch absorbed avant-garde influences from Conner and Brakhage. Indeed, Lynch's depiction of BOB entering our world out of the swirling, multicolored quantum fog of the Trinity detonation bears an undeniable resemblance to the opening sequences of Brakhage's legendary *Dog Star Man; Part I* (1962), in which the primordial title character (played by Brakhage himself) materializes suddenly out of the murky warping and flaring swirls of color constituting the film's diegesis to that point. The man appears in a wooded landscape that has congealed from a universe in quantum flux just moments before; he is bearded, carries an axe over his shoulder, and wears a heavy flannel shirt. In his abstract and highly impressionistic fashion, Brakhage shows us the human form—the anthropos as primeval humanity, which Gnostics referred to as the Adamas—separating itself from its encompassing environment, emerging from its gestation, materializing in a fashion not unlike BOB's appearance within the Trinity detonation. What we are offered in each instance is an aesthetic archetype of the anthropos; while Brackhage allows us to consider the anthropos as the primeval Adamas achieving its differentiation from the environment that created it—and carrying an axe that portends the human propensity for altering that environment—Lynch provides us with a rendering of the Ahramanic anthropos, completely inimical to the beings and worlds it encounters, in the figure of BOB.[6]

Like Brackhage, Lynch has long been a meticulous visual stylist, and his talents come across clearly in the nuclear aesthetics at the center of "Gotta Light?" Especially striking in terms of this discussion of Conner and Brakhage is Lynch's decision to shoot the Trinity and Woodsman sequence in black and white, which not only matches the color palette of *Crossroads* and *23rd Psalm Branch* but also matches our filmic and visual past more generally. When viewers continue to experience the devious machinations and effects of BOB, the Woodsman, and the frog-moths in the colored present of *Twin Peaks*, they are reminded that the forces released in the past cannot be relegated to or contained within that temporal frame—they continue to contaminate the here and now—and that seems to be entirely the point, a point which mirrors the Atomic

Art of experimental filmmakers such as Conner and Brakhage.

Androcentrism

While my focus thus far has been on "Gotta Light?", ecological or environmental perspectives abound through *Twin Peaks* from the outset—right from the opening credits actually, as the initial shot of a perching Bewick's Wren dissolves into the smokestacks of the Packard Mill splitting the wren's forest environment into lumber. The next shot takes us inside the mill, revealing a mechanized saw sharpener honing a circular saw for the processing of Douglas firs. Lynch's camera then takes us out again into the surrounding environs, starting with a stunning shot of the Snoqualmie Falls that fades into a shot of the languidly flowing Snoqualmie River. Moving from the inner workings of the mill to the scenic splendors of Washington State's Snoqualmie Valley, Lynch's shot sequence offers us a fairly conventional nature-based and romantic perspective on ecology, juxtaposing the beauty of the forest and its waterways to the industrialized machinery consuming its resources. Ultimately, Lynch also connects this predation to the emergence of the atomic age in provocative ways.

Twin Peaks is a narrative that begins with a female corpse—just as each episode begins with the forest being industrially processed into lumber. Much like the region's Douglas firs, Laura has been cut down. Laura's murder at the hands of BOB, who has long possessed Laura's father, Leland, comes only after she has been exposed to all manner of sexual exploitation, violence, and malfeasance. Laura's female body is fundamentally linked to the forest in their shared and destructive exploitation. Again, the opening credits stress this connection, as **the murdered Laura's yearbook photo is superimposed over the lush Pacific Northwest forests under the threat of the local mill saw.** This point is also reinforced in the series' iconic Red Room, an extradimensional waiting room connecting the forest to other dimensions within the *Twin Peaks* multiverse, where the murdered Laura appears on more than one occasion alongside a statue of Venus, Roman goddess of fertility. Moreover, in "Gotta Light?" two otherworldly characters known as the Fireman and Señorita Dido—housed in a fortress in one of those parallel but interlinked realms—send an orb containing Laura's essence to Earth in order to counter the orb containing BOB (released into the world at the Trinity site) in what is best described as a Manichean interdimensional struggle. Earth has become a battleground in that struggle with Laura serving as an archetype for female purity who becomes defiled, then ultimately meets her destruction in the earthly dimension (much like the forest wilderness to which she is so powerfully and consistently linked).

Laura is not the only female character perilously linked to the fate of the forest. Just as season 1 begins with the death of Laura, season 2 ends with the victimization of Annie Blackburn, who has just been crowned Miss Twin Peaks. Annie, a principled seeker and religious outsider who has recently spent five years in a convent, arrives in Twin Peaks during the second half of season 2, and soon becomes Dale Cooper's love interest. Cooper is of course the protagonist of *Twin Peaks* and its most iconic character. An eccentric FBI agent with an interest in Tibetan Buddhism and esoteric metaphysics, Cooper has been sent to Twin Peaks to lead Laura's murder investigation, though his attention is diverted to one of the central plotlines of the second season, involving the Ghostwood Development Project, which has designs on building a country club in Twin Peak's fictional Ghostwood National Forest—and Annie eventually becomes one of the most important voices in the Stop Ghostwood campaign.

With the hope of thwarting the development project, the Stop Ghostwood campaign focuses much of its organizing effort on the fate of the local pine weasel, mirroring real world concerns over the Northern Spotted Owl, placed under the protection of the Endangered Species Act in June 1990 (contemporaneous with the shooting of season 2). A modest-sized raptor, the Spotted Owl provided a mobilizing cause for that era's environmentalism, its existence threatened by widespread clear-cut logging from Northern California to the Pacific Northwest in which *Twin Peaks* is set. Benjamin Horn spearheads the Stop Ghostwood campaign. Long a cutthroat and highly unprincipled local businessman—a complete reprobate, scoundrel, and misogynist, really—Horn experiences a change of heart following an extended mental breakdown spanning the middle of season 2 and emerges with a revivified moral conscience that he retains through the episodes of the return season. As Ben explains to the attendees of a fundraising fashion show for Stop Ghostwood during episode 17 of the second season: "The Stop Ghostwood campaign is a determined effort to keep the rabid development interests from trying to turn our beautiful Northwest forests into a monstrous amusement park, destroying animal preserves which have been undisturbed for centuries, the little worlds that serve as sanctums for several endangered species," including, of course, the pine weasel.

Ben establishes the Miss Twin Peaks contest to raise additional funds for Stop Ghostwood. Despite her reluctance to enter a pageant she rightly views as degrading, Annie is crowned Miss Twin Peaks (in season 2, episode 21) after a stirring speech in which she first quotes Chief Seattle, then insists that her audience more fully embrace ecological responsibility. Learning to be more responsible residents of the planet, Annie explains, will require a sea change, a fundamental shift in our day-to-day thinking toward prioritizing ecological issues. She closes by imploring, "let us, in walking gently upon the earth, leave behind a simple legacy: that we're new warriors, mystic warriors, who love the earth, and try to save it." Chaos ensues at the conclusion of Annie's speech, as Wyndham Earl, Cooper's psychopathic former FBI partner, abducts Annie, and pilots her away to the Red Room in Glastonbury Grove (though Earl refers to the Red Room as the Black Lodge, a designation he has borrowed from local Native American mythology). Earl hopes to lure Cooper to the lodge in order to destroy him, though Earl's grand plan involves releasing malevolent interdimensional forces that will destroy Twin Peaks and the Earthly realm. While Annie ultimately escapes the Red Room/Black Lodge she is reduced to a catatonic state and never returns to play an active role in the Twin Peaks narrative. The trauma of Annie's abduction fully destroys her mental capacities and silences her.

Ben and Annie's entreaties regarding the ecosystem are undeniably earnest and impactful and the ensuing destruction of Annie is consistent with Lynch's longtime interests in the roots and consequences of misogynistic violence. Sherryl Vint suggests that the emergence of ecocriticism and animal studies in the years since the airing of the original series provides lenses that reveal how "images of animals and nature in *Twin Peaks* are deeply enmeshed in the series' meditation upon the inevitable loss of innocence to encroaching modernity," a loss witnessed in the destruction of Annie (71). Moreover, in identifying the Trinity detonation with the birth of BOB—the Ahramanic anthropos who irradiates the world and murders Laura—Lynch connects the anthropogenic depravity characteristic of encroaching modernity to male depravity, or to androcentrism, in which presumably inherent male capabilities for domination over women are mirrored in male assumptions about the human right to dominate hierarchically over the natural world. Crowning Annie Miss Twin Peaks foregrounds the androcentric perspective and perhaps asks us to consider the extent to which movements for ecological justice, such as Stop Ghostwood, can act in complicity with the feminization of the natural world. In Laura's murder, in Annie's abduction and trauma, and in the unauthorized penetration of the sleeping female form by the frog-moth, the forces involved in violating female bodies and the forces threatening the destruction of our lifeworld are often, in *Twin Peaks*, one and the same.

 This connection comes across powerfully in episode 11 of the return season, "There's Fire Where You Are Going." At a pivotal moment in that episode, Gordon Cole stands before an interdimensional portal in the Midwestern United States—a swirling vortex in the sky much like the one through which BOB enters the Earthly dimension—

and sees what he identifies as "dirty bearded men" descending a staircase. These figures are other woodsmen, sooty attendants of BOB, and in light of the engagement with and critique of androcentric perspectives at the heart of Twin Peaks, it seems particularly apt to point out that "dirty" is simultaneously a synonym for perversion, defilement, and contamination.

With their grimy visages—which appear to be smeared with coal and oil—along with their lumberjack clothes, Lynch's woodsmen are clearly a composite symbol of human energy extraction, or fuel history, from lumber to coal to oil to the fission event that ushered them into our realm. They are the sullied (or shadow) counterparts to Brackhage's Adamas in *Dog Star Man*, and after they emerge during the "Gotta Light?" episode the woodsmen gather around a gas station in the New Mexican desert that serves them as a headquarters of sorts. Moreover, on multiple occasions over the course of the series, characters claim to have smelled oil, "scorched engine oil" in those locations where acts of male violence have occurred. The smell of scorched oil of course suggests mechanicity and fossil fuel consumption, but it is also the smell that emanates from heated, working chainsaws, such as those used to cut down the northwestern forest (and Laura metaphorically). There is also a large pool of burnt engine oil in the middle of the sycamore grove that serves as the portal to the Red Room or Black Lodge, through which Wyndham takes Annie. Earlier during that same episode (the concluding episode of season two), another character, Margaret "The Log Lady" Lanterman, brings Cooper a mason jar of used motor oil, informing him that "this oil is an opening to a gateway."[7]

Lynch suggests through such details that the detonation at Trinity had androcentric precursors in a longer history of environmental destruction and fuel extraction, an observation that resonates powerfully with Werner Heisenberg's remarks on organized energy extraction and the dawning of the Anthropocene (though Heisenberg does not explicitly call it that): "The great expansion of [the] combination of natural and technical science started when one had succeeded in putting some of the forces of nature at the disposal of man. The energy stored in coal, for instance, could then perform some of the work which formerly had to be done by man himself" (163). Heisenberg goes on to observe that "Modern physics belongs to the most recent parts of this development, and its unfortunately most visible result, the invention of nuclear weapons, has shown the essence of this development in the sharpest possible light" (164). What Heisenberg finds so alarming about the "essence of this development" is the possibility that we will not be able to control what we have unleashed, just as the world created by Lynch in *Twin Peaks* struggles to rein in the unleashed anthropos figured as BOB and his grimy underlings. Again, in Heisenberg's own words, "Undoubtedly the process [of organized energy extraction] has fundamentally changed the conditions of life on our earth; and whether one approves of it or not, whether one calls it progress or danger, one must realize that it has gone far beyond any control through human forces," though those anthropogenic and androcentric forces were its catalyst (163).

The human ability to consciously alter matter at the elemental level—a fundamental characteristic of the

Anthropocene—is exemplified by the transmuting of nuclei under laboratory conditions, a process which birthed nuclear physics as a discipline and made atomic weaponry possible. Some have pointed out that these pursuits have always been possessed by androcentric motivations. As Decamous proclaims in *Invisible Colors* for instance: "Virginia Woolf, and in her footsteps Susan Sontag, previously emphasized that war has a gender, and it is male. The nuclear industry has one too. It is (mainly) male—or rather heterosexual male" (291). Much of what transpires in "Gotta Light?" and in *Twin Peaks* more generally offers a similar critique of the androcentric roots of atomism. Indeed, even Heisenberg, in his use of penetration language, might be accused of describing the scientific relationship to the natural world in androcentric language: "The penetration of science into the more remote parts of nature enabled the engineers to use forces of nature which in former periods had scarcely been known" (163).

Cosmological Violence

We should also consider the significance of Lynch's bearded "dirty" men in specific relation to the history of resource extraction in the southwestern United States, where so much of "Gotta Light?" is set. Particularly helpful in this regard is "Our Homeland, A National Sacrifice Area," a work of literary Atomic Art by Acoma writer Simon Ortiz, combining poetry, autobiography, and historical narrative into an exploration of the troubling relationship between Indigenous peoples in New Mexico and the industrial and governmental entities responsible for predatory uranium mining and the development of the first atomic weapons. Consider Ortiz's description of the decimation of sacred desert landscapes at the hands of mining entities such as Anaconda Copper: "The Anaconda engineers surveyed and plotted, and soon they drilled the stone, filled the drill holes with dynamite, and blasted. And pushed the rubble away. They did it over and over again, until the land was just so much rubble pushed aside to find the strata of uranium bearing ore" (355). Indeed, we might say that even prior to the Trinity detonation the desert landscapes venerated by southwestern Indigenous peoples were being drilled and blasted into the Anthropocene by androcentric forces. Moreover, the drilling and blasting for uranium was preceded by a more extensive period of violent resource extraction (also by machine and blasting). Again, as Ortiz explains, "There were any number of explorations for uranium since the 1940's in New Mexico. Oil, gas, and coal had been found and developed on the Navajo homeland since the 1920's, and it was common knowledge that they were profitable to exploit because of their location and the ready supply of labor" (353-54). Along with this extraction of fossil fuels, logging companies also laid siege to the area beginning in the 1920s, cutting down whatever trees they could find while killing animals indiscriminately in order to feed the inhabitants of the logging camps in the New Mexican desert (Silko 172).

Considered in relation to this history, the appearance of Lynch's bearded men out of the New Mexican desert, dressed in lumberjack attire, faces smeared with oily soot, makes a great deal of sense. In episode 11 of the return season, "There is Fire Where You're Going," Gordon Cole first refers to these henchmen of BOB as "dirty bearded men," as a composite symbol of androcentric resource extraction. During that same episode, Deputy Chief Tommy "Hawk" Hill, a Nez Perce (or Nimiipuu), shares an ancient tribal map of the wilderness surrounding Twin Peaks with Sheriff Truman, hoping to shed some metaphysical light on BOB and related events. Explaining that "this map is very old but is always current," Hawk shows the sheriff "Blue Pine Mountain—a very revered sacred site," a site of cosmological significance to his people. At the base of the mountain as represented on Hawk's map is a fire symbol, which he explains represents "a type of fire," closer in its meaning to energy or "modern day electricity." When asked by Truman if the fire symbol represents something positive or negative, Hawk replies that it "depends upon the intention, the intention behind the fire." Hawk's point that the meaning of energy/fire depends on the intentions of its user is the very same point made in Indigenous and New Mexican writings about the extraction and enrichment of uranium. By extension, the goals, assumptions, and stratagems of the Manhattan Project might easily be likened to the intentions of Wyndham Earl in attempting to open the extradimensional portal (also marked on Hawk's map) to negative entities. Earl enters as a malignancy into the spirit world contained within the tribal map and as such represents the same type of malevolent forces who have historically used Native American sacred sites and uranium toward exceedingly negative and ill-conceived ends. Such intentions are also represented on Hawk's map as "black fire," the fire of death.

In Leslie Marmon Silko's monumental work of Atomic Art, the novel *Ceremony*, she observes that "Up here / in these hills / they will find the rocks, / rocks with veins of green and yellow and black, / They will lay the final pattern with these rocks / they will lay it across the world / and explode everything" (127). Those involved in refining and enriching mined uranium into an instrument of death, into "black fire," had, according to Silko, intentionally manipulated and perverted the natural world toward Ahrimanic ends. As southwestern historian E.A. Mares so eloquently points out in "Los Alamos: Coming Down from the Hill of Certainty," the development of atomic weapons in New Mexico involved a great deal of callous disregard and violence toward Indigenous sacred traditions and cosmology from the outset. Los Alamos National Laboratory was founded during the Second World War for the purpose of developing nuclear weaponry, and two of the weapons created there incinerated much of Hiroshima and Nagasaki, roughly three weeks after the Trinity detonation. Writing of the lab's founding, Mares shares some legitimate "reservations about how Los Alamos National Laboratory (LANL) has historically related to its surrounding communities in Northern New Mexico. These are primarily, although not entirely, Pueblo Indian or Hispanic communities" (48). Indeed, Mares wonders if Robert Oppenheimer and Lieutenant General Leslie Groves, while driving through the Jemez River Valley in 1942 to scout the site for the laboratory, cared at all "that they were following the path of a sacred river. They were crossing a territory populated by people of ancient cultures who possessed an utterly different world view" (51). Of course, the evidence suggests that they did not care at all, as Groves, Oppenheimer, and others used the veil of secrecy around the project to leave the local population entirely out of the decision-making process regarding the

98 • Todd Tietchen

location of the lab and ultimately the detonation at Trinity, the false dawn which caught the inhabitants of the area entirely by surprise.

In addressing the history of cultural disregard and cosmological violence enacted by colonial forces and the occupying U.S. government—the militarized arm of Western modernity—Laguna Pueblo writer Paula Gunn Allen employs apocalyptic language resonant with the concept of the *Ahrimanic anthropos*. Indigenous sacred sites and traditions, as Gunn Allen observes, have most often been violated by "the horsemen of the Apocalypse who thunder through [Indigenous] environs attempting by war, plague, famine, and pestilence to destroy [them]. Why is it that the United States armed forces have a bombing range in a Hawaiian island once filled with temples and holy sites? Do they seriously believe that bombs can destroy the gods?" (9). Gunn Allen is referencing the island of Kahoʻolawe, home of the sea god Kamaloa, which the United States used indiscriminately as a bombing range for decades. Gunn Allen's observation reminds us that weapons testing and its aftermaths most often represent a heartless disregard for the natural world, which is simultaneously a mode of cosmological violence—a desecration of the living planet and the sacred simultaneously. Indeed, the decision to name the 1956 detonations of Operation Redwing after Indigenous tribes can only be seen from this perspective as the darkest mode of sarcasm, the bleakest irony.

In *Ceremony*, Silko refers to the malignant and impious forces behind cosmological violence and atomic destruction as "the witchery," the ghastly arts of "the destroyers." In writing of the Trinity detonation, Silko imparts that from "that time on, human beings were one clan again, united by the fate the destroyers had planned for all of them, for all living things; united by a circle of death that devoured people in cities twelve thousand miles away, victims who had never known these mesas, who had never seen the delicate colors of the rocks which boiled up their slaughter" (228). The new era ushered in at the Trinity blast site might of course be identified as the Anthropocene, the ushering of planetary life into newly immense and calamitous possibilities not fully contained within the local. Again, the destroyers are the *Ahriman*, the shadow figure of western rationality and its confident claims to progress. In this instance, Silko reminds us that detonations are local traumas with nonlocal repercussions. The false sun transfigured our planetary precarity into a powerful symbol of anthropogenic and androcentric doom. Lynch's own perspective resonates notably in this instance with these Indigenous perspectives.

Post-Nature

In the Anthropocene, we come to inhabit expansive and fatal proximities. As Silko shows us, detonations are local traumas with nonlocal repercussions in the form of radionuclide fallout and the heightened sense of universal precarity that attends post-Hiroshima times—or our present in the Anthropocene. This recognition—inspired in Silko's case by the extent to which the realities of atomic devastation and its effects come to touch "all living things"—undergirds post-nature theoretical approaches to ecology. As Timothy Clark has observed, in post-nature approaches "what was once the nature/culture distinction" orienting classical environmentalism and first-wave ecocriticism "becomes [refigured as] the incalculable interaction of imponderable contaminated, hybrid elements with unpredictable emergent effects" (80). From within the midst of anthropogenically altered—and perhaps irreparably compromised—ecologies, there emerges "an incalculable connection between bodies, human and nonhuman, across and within the biosphere (food, water, nutrients, but also toxins and viruses), with a sense of both holism and, increasingly, entrapment" (80). Members of Silko's "one clan," we encounter these incalculable connections as a "loss of externality," a radical internality measurable in part by the accumulation of toxic materials and carcinogens such as heavy metals and glyphosate in our own bodily tissues, or in the threat of viral outbreaks such as we are currently experiencing with COVID 19.

Twin Peaks: The Return compels us to consider these harmful, viscous forces, the dangerous and deadly intimacies between human and nonhuman entities such as pesticides, residual radioactive materials, and all sorts of pollution and contamination. The return season of *Twin Peaks* does not revive the narrative arc involving Stop Ghostwood, and in general the forest is less emphasized during the third season as a setting or character. Defilement and contamination, however, remain fundamental interests of Lynch, with Dr. Amp serving as their mouthpiece. Dr. Amp is the alias or stage name for Dr. Lawrence Jacoby, featured in seasons 1 and 2 as Laura's unconventional and deeply troubling psychiatrist. Like most of the other men in Laura's life, Dr. Jacoby fails her. Their therapeutic relationship becomes fatally clouded by erotic transference, and Jacoby seems to have encouraged

Laura's riskier behavior for his own voyeuristic reasons. Following Laura's murder, Jacoby is stripped of his license on account of their inappropriate therapeutic relationship, which has contributed to Laura's destruction.

While the character of Dr. Jacoby was initially based on famed ethnobotanist and psychonaut Terence McKenna, Dr. Amp now appears as some cross between McKenna, Madame Psychosis of David Foster Wallace's *Infinite Jest*, and Zach Bush. In his persona as a radicalized podcaster, he proffers an inchoate politics amalgamated from alt-right conspiracies, the rhetoric of Occupy Wall Street, folk populism, and left-leaning libertarianism. One of his primary concerns, however, is with ecology, though his perspective is clearly post-nature. While Ben Horn's ecological awakening involves protecting the wilderness from predatory developers, Dr. Amp tells us, in episode 5 of the return season, that the totality of our environment is already "poisoned," contributing to ever increasing rates of "cancer, leukemia, autoimmune disorders." We now encounter ecological crisis not only in the forests, deserts, and oceans but also in the kernel of ourselves, within our permeable physiology. When Dr. Amp warns us that "our air, our water, our earth, the very soil itself, our food, our bodies, [are] poisoned," that "they're poisoning us!" with mercury, fluoride, and other toxins, he is addressing viscosity, the potential of heavy metals, radiation, and other toxins to stick to and penetrate us—which is to say, their capacity for becoming radically internal like BOB and the frog-moths.[8]

Moreover, post-nature ecological perspectives have played an integral role in the Lynchian aesthetic since the director's first feature-length film, *Eraserhead*, which emphasizes that the human form has already become possessed by the alien and the toxic—its core has already been pierced by ineffably stubborn malignancies resistant to containment. Inspired by Lynch's own experiences of the industrial afterlife of late 1960s Philadelphia, where Lynch was enrolled in the Pennsylvania Academy of Fine Arts, *Eraserhead*, according to Dennis Lim, is "a story of failed procreation within a landscape of defunct industry [that] links machinery and biology from the get-go, as a scarred demiurge (the credits call him the Man in the Planet) pulls a lever that propels a giant spermatozoon into the cosmos" (35). The beginning of the film mirrors the birth of BOB in "Gotta Light?" then addresses post-nature ecology in ways consistent with *Twin Peaks: The Return*. Set in the postindustrial wasteland that Henry, the protagonist, calls home, *Eraserhead* renders the issue of human fertility monstrous. Henry's lover, Mary X, has given birth to some sort of mutated creature with a snakelike head, only faintly resembling a human baby, and ultimately their progeny dies on account of its lacking skin and a skeletal system to protect its internal organs. *Eraserhead* stresses that our continued reproduction as a species has become fraught within a polluted and contaminated world, and in this way the film anticipates the death of Laura Palmer—the only child of Sarah and Leland Palmer, brutalized and murdered by Leland (who is possessed or infected by BOB). As Lim also observes, the mushroom cloud in *Eraserhead* actually explodes from Henry's head, his hairstyle an iconic representation of Atomic Art, much like Bruce Conner's painting, *Bombhead* (1989) (40). Indeed, as Ashlee Joyce has already pointed out, "the framed photograph of the Trinity nuclear test that appears in *Eraserhead* over the nightstand in Henry Spencer's bachelor apartment is the same photograph" as the one framed on the wall of Cole's FBI office (15). These elements establish Henry as a representative figure of post-Hiroshima times, or of the Anthropocene, signaling his own contamination.

One of the primary influences on *Eraserhead* was *The Metamorphosis* (1915), and its author, Franz Kafka, makes a thematically weighty appearance in *Twin Peaks: The Return* (Lim 123). Late in episode 3 of the return season, "Call for Help," we are shown Gordon Cole's office in the J. Edgar Hoover building (which houses the FBI). Behind Gordon's desk is the enormous photographic print of the Trinity detonation and on the wall facing his desk is a photographic reproduction of Kafka. Composed during WWI, *The Metamorphosis* obviously insinuates that modernity involves the toxic or monstrous habitation of the human, an insinuation that casts a long shadow of influence over Lynch's work. Kafka was a prophet of our anti-transfiguration—our integration with the nonhuman in the Anthropocene—as the overnight transformation of Gregor Samsa into a human-sized insect acknowledges that we are not bodily sealed within anthropocentric uniqueness. Perhaps another way of saying this is that Kafka dramatizes the moment in which the anthropos awakens to discover that it is no better than an insect within the planetary scheme of things—a realization not without its share of despair and estrangement for Gregor (and for Kafka evidently). As Dr. Amp also understands, in modernity we might as well forget about being transfigured into the divine, as the bodily form becomes trapped in or serves as the container for inescapable, though barely comprehended, toxicities and mutations.

The consequences of anthropogenic activity—including deforestation, pollution, fossil fuel economies, and nuclear fallout—have triggered ecological processes that shall prove exceedingly difficult, if not impossible, to contain. All of these consequences find expression in *Twin Peaks*, where they are linked powerfully to the transmutation of nuclei that allows for the detonation of atomic weapons (at a tremendous cost to Earthen life and environments). Ashlee Joyce suggests that in "Gotta Light?" **Lynch asks us to "take stock of nuclear armaments' continued repercussions,"** decades after Francis Fukuyama famously declared an end to the Cold War and history itself (14). Moreover, the return season "revisits the connection between our neoliberal present and the nuclear past by way of the image of the detonation of the first atomic bomb— depicting it as an exceptional event that constitutes nothing less than the birth of contemporary evil" (22). In this essay I have been asking us to name that "evil" more precisely as our advancing state of precarity within the **Anthropocene.** As Heisenberg realized, "the penetration of science into the more remote parts of nature" represented a potentially world-annihilating culmination of human efforts to harness the forces of the natural world for energy and other means, as humans began to consciously alter matter at its fundamental level. Heisenberg's history of potentially disastrous human resource endeavoring finds potent expression in the origin story of BOB, the Woodsmen, and the hatchlings—along with the title of episode 8 of the return season, "Gotta Light?" Lynch's choice of this **Promethean title situates the underpinnings of the Anthropocene in deeper time,** somewhere back in the mysterious origins of human technical life when we initially became the anthropos, when we first became capable of altering our biophysical environments and ecosystems to suit our immediate needs at the cost of our future.

Notes

1. It should be pointed out that Lynch collaborated with television writer and novelist Mark Frost on the first two seasons of *Twin Peaks*. Lynch also allowed some other directors to direct individual episodes, which is fairly common in television production. Frost did not collaborate (beyond an executive producer credit) on the 1992 film *Twin Peaks: Fire Walk with Me*, on which Lynch shared writing credits with Robert Engels. While Frost returned as a co-writer on *The Return* season, Lynch himself directed every episode.

2. Over the past two decades, the term *Anthropocene* has come to signal a new sequence of planetary time indicated by accelerating and alarming human influence over the earth's climatic systems. In the Anthropocene, we become ecological and geological agents capable of causing environmental damage of great and lasting magnitude. As used in geology, the term *golden spike* refers to a geologic marker indicating significant changes in the geologic record, and the AWP views the increased presence of radionuclides in planetary stratigraphy as irrefutable evidence of a significant human-induced change. Of course, Nobel Prize winning chemist Paul Crutzen coined the term Anthropocene to account for the human-induced stresses to planetary systems that begin to appear during the First Industrial Revolution, though Crutzen has also specified that the Anthropocene evolves from its larval to its advanced and more momentous stage after 1945, a period he refers to as the "Great Acceleration." Others posit the onset of the Anthropocene in deeper time, aligning its genesis with the emergence of simple

human tools 2.6 million years ago, or with the development of human agriculture 12,000 years ago (which required the clearing of forests). Currently, a single model accounting for the origins of the Anthropocene has yet to achieve clear dominance. See Jeremy Davies, *The Birth of the Anthropocene* (University of California Press, 2018), 41-69.

3. See this Reddit thread for instance: https://www.reddit.com/r/twinpeaks/comments/6vplfb/s3e14_sarah_palmer_the_frog_moth_and_the_jumping/

4. See Paul Boyer, "The United States, 1941–1963: A Historical Overview," *Vital Forms: American Art and Design in the Atomic Age, 1940–1960*, Ed. Brooke Kamin Rapaport and Kevin L. Stayton (New York: Harry N. Abrams, 2001), 32-60; and Todd F. Tietchen, *Technomodern Poetics: The American Literary Avant-Garde at the Start of the Information Age* (Iowa City: University of Iowa Press, 2018), 59-79.

5. As such, the film might easily be read as a meditation on what Crutzen later terms the Great Acceleration.

6. My thinking about these archetypes has been highly influenced by Carl Jung and C.S. Lewis, along with a number of Native American writers to be discussed in the essay proper. Jung discusses two symbolic manifestations or archetypes of the anthropos in *Flying Saucers*, Routledge, 2002. First published in 1958, *Flying Saucers* explores the psychological and archetypal roots of the UFO phenomena of the 1950s. According to Jung, descriptions and accounts of UFOs (which are of course uniquely Anthropocene narratives) correspond at times to the "image of the divine-human personality, the Primordial Man, or Anthropos" (17). This is the Adamas in the Gnostic sense, symbolizing newness and renewal. At other times, the content of UFO narratives resonate with the "figure of the *homo maximus*," an archetype possessed by demonic and numinous propensities simultaneously, capable of both doom and subsequent renewal (90). Moreover, Jung relates this archetype to the concerns of the twentieth-century avant-garde which "has given expression to

the fundamental fear of our age—the catastrophic outbreak of destructive forces which everyone dreads" (83). Dada, Expressionism, and other modes of postwar abstraction provide terrifying shape to "our catastrophic age," giving expression to the "conscious and unconscious will for destruction [and depicting] the collapse of our civilization in chaos" (83).

My own designation of the *Ahrimanic anthropos* (from the Zoroastrian and Gnostic entity, Ahriman, the lord of destruction and strife) attempts to address the propensities for destruction and chaos inherent in human civilization in a less equivocal manner than Jung's *homo maximus*, and bears a debt to C.S. Lewis's Space Trilogy. The physicist Dr. Weston serves as the primary antagonist of the first two books in that trilogy, *Out of the Silent Planet* (1938) and *Perelandra* (1943). *Out of the Silent Planet* is set principally on Mars, a planet whose inhabitants Weston views (through his anthropocentrism) as naturally inferior to humans and thus suited for subjugation. Weston is a galactic imperialist who imagines humanity hopping from planet to planet out into the vast expanses of the Milky Way, using each planet's resources—and conquering their indigenous populations—as it goes. The following book, *Perelandra*, takes place predominantly on Venus, and over the course of its narrative Weston the physicist physically transforms into an Ahrimanic or demonic entity, using his new razor-sharp claws to dissect Venus's amphibious and avian creatures and to discard them as if they were garbage across the planet's surface. He is counterposed to the *Adamas* in the form of Venus's first *anthropoi*, the planet's Adam and Eve, who possess an innately utopian conception of their relationship to the Venusian ecology and must now face down their tempter in the *Ahrimanic* form of Weston, the conscienceless consumer of planets whose cold rationality operates at a pronounced spiritual deficiency.

7. Margaret Lanterman, who always carries a small log in her arm and has thus become known as the Log Lady, is another female character connected to the forest. Margaret has a psychic

connection to the log and serves as a medium for its messages. The log possesses a consciousness that Margaret honors, and like any sage or esoteric seeker, she has a penchant for relaying the log's messages in the form of riddles and non-sequiturs. Over the course of *Twin Peaks*, Margaret's panpsychic connection to her log allows her to access metaphysical knowledge much as a clairvoyant might have used a crystal ball to scry.

8. I think that it is important to point out that in post-nature ecological perspectives, such as Dr. Amp's, it is not as if the pollution and contamination of the wilderness is no longer an issue. That's not really what post-nature means. Instead, such perspectives ask us to acknowledge the ubiquity of environmental pollution as it touches all of our ecologies and human societies—how it comes to touch us in all of the places where we live—rather than focusing on the forest, the ocean, and other ecologies that we identify with the wild or the natural world. Another way of saying this is that post-nature approaches expand the purviews of ecological thinking rather than completely superseding longstanding environmental concerns with wilderness or the wild. These are not exclusive viewpoints, as Lynch shows us over the course of *Twin Peaks* in its entirety, and for him nature-based and post-nature ecology share a common nemesis in androcentrism.

Works Cited

23rd Psalm Branch. Directed by Stan Brakhage, Canyon Cinema, 1967.

Adams, Sam. "With a Surreal Flashback, Twin Peaks Rewrote the Rules of TV, Again." *Slate*, 26 June 2017, https://slate.com/culture/2017/06/twin-peaks-part-8-is-one-of-the-most-radical-hours-of-tv-ever.html. Accessed 20 May 2021.

"Beyond Life and Death." *Twin Peaks*, created by David Lynch and Mark Frost, season 2, episode 22, ABC, 1991.

"Call for Help." *Twin Peaks: The Return*, created by David

Lynch and Mark Frost, episode 3, Rancho Rosa Partnership and Showtime, 2017.
"Case Files." *Twin Peaks: The Return*, created by David Lynch and Mark Frost, episode 5, Rancho Rosa Partnership and Showtime, 2017.
Clark, Timothy. "Nature, Post Nature." *The Cambridge Companion to Literature and the Environment*, edited by Louise Westling Cambridge University Press, 2014, pp. 75-89.
Crossroads. Directed by Bruce Connor, Canyon Cinema, 1976.
Davies, Jeremy. *The Birth of the Anthropocene*. University of California Press, 2018.
Decamous, Gabrielle. *Invisible Colors: The Arts of the Atomic Age*. MIT Press, 2018.
Dog Star Man. Directed by Stan Brakhage, Canyon Cinema, 1964.
Ghosh, Amitav. *The Great Derangement: Climate Change and the Unthinkable*. University of Chicago Press, 2016.
Godzilla. Directed by Ishirō Honda, Toho Studios, 1954.
"Gotta Light?" *Twin Peaks: The Return*, created by David Lynch and Mark Frost, episode 8, Rancho Rosa Partnership and Showtime, 2017.
Gunn Allen, Paula. *Grandmothers of the Light: A Medicine Woman's Sourcebook*. Boston: Beacon Press, 1992.
Heisenberg, Werner. *Physics and Philosophy: The Revolution in Modern Science*. Harper Perennial, 2007.
Joyce, Ashlee. "The Nuclear Anxiety of *Twin Peaks: The Return*," *The Politics of* Twin Peaks, ed. Amanda DiPaolo and Jamie Gillies, Lanham/Boulder/New York/London: Lexington Books (2019): 13-34.
Lim, Dennis. *David Lynch: The Man From Another Place*. Amazon Publishing, 2015.
Mares, E.A. "Los Alamos: Coming Down from the Hill of Certainty." *New Mexico Historical Review* 72 (January 1997): 47-56.

"Miss Twin Peaks." *Twin Peaks*, created by David Lynch and Mark Frost, season 2, episode 21, ABC, 1991.

Morton, Timothy. *Hyperobjects: Philosophy and Ecology after the End of the World*. Minneapolis: University of Minnesota Press, 2013.

"No Knock, No Doorbell." *Twin Peaks: The Return*, created by David Lynch and Mark Frost, episode 16, Rancho Rosa Partnership and Showtime, 2017.

Ortiz, Simon J. "Our Homeland, A National Sacrifice Area." *Woven Stone*. Tucson and London: University of Arizona Press, 1992. 337-63.

"The Past Dictates the Future." *Twin Peaks: The Return*, created by David Lynch and Mark Frost, episode 17, Rancho Rosa Partnership and Showtime, 2017.

Silko, Leslie Marmon. *Ceremony*. New York: Penguin, 2006.

Sanders, Robert. "Was First Nuclear Test the Start of the New Human-Dominated Epoch, the Anthropocene?" *Berkeley News*, 16 January 2015, news.berkeley.edu/2015/01/16/was-first-nuclear-test-dawn-of-new-human-dominated-epoch-the-anthropocene/. Accessed 3 June 2019.

Stamhuis, Lindsay. "Destroyer of Worlds: Nuclear Fallout in the World of Twin Peaks." *25YL*, 30 June 2017, https://25yearslatersite.com/2017/06/30/destroyer-of-worlds-nuclear-fallout-in-the-world-of-twin-peaks/. Accessed 20 May 2021.

Subramanian, Meera. "Anthropocene Now: Influential Panel Votes to Recognize Earth's New Epoch." *Nature*, 21 May 2019, www.nature.com/articles/d41586-019-01641-5. Accessed 3 June 2019.

"There's Fire Where You Are Going." *Twin Peaks: The Return*, created by David Lynch and Mark Frost, episode 11, Rancho Rosa Partnership and Showtime, 2017.

Vidal, John. "Are Coastal Nuclear Power Plants Ready for Sea Level Rise?" *Hakai Magazine*, 21 August 2018, www.hakaimagazine.com/features/are-coastal-nuclear-power-plants-ready-for-sea-level-rise/. Accessed 7 July 2019.

Vint, Sherryl. "'The Owls Are Not What They Seem': Animals and Nature in *Twin Peaks*," *Return to Twin Peaks: New Approaches to Materiality, Theory, and Genre on Television*, ed. Jeffrey Andrew Weinstock and Catherine Spooner, NY: Palgrave Macmillan (2016): 71-86.

"What is your Name?" *Twin Peaks: The Return*, created by David Lynch and Mark Frost, episode 18, Rancho Rosa Partnership and Showtime, 2017.

"Wounds and Scars." *Twin Peaks*, created by David Lynch and Mark Frost, season 2, episode 17, ABC, 1991.

Han Song's Weirdly Sublime Anti-Modernity

Ron Judy

> Absurdity penned by Chinese science-fiction writers is different from the absurdity of Kafka. It is a habit acquired through five thousand years of civilization and has strong national characteristics....I myself can often sense this absurdity growing and spreading through everyday life and this is one important reason why I write. Wrapped in the most sacred of clothing, it works its way into the very bones of life and society....and then from ordinary citizens to the interests of the state, it can be betrayed and sacrificed amid a righteous, knowing silence.
>
> --Han Song[1]

CONTEMPORARY CRITICS of Chinese science fiction have tended to trace its genealogy back to the late-Qing Dynasty and May Fourth eras—and specifically to the works of Liang Qi-chao and Lu Xun. The latter's influential translation of Jules Verne's "Journey to the Moon" (Yuejie lvxing, 1903), and Liang's science fictional tale "A Record of the Future of New China" (1902) are thought to be the starting-points of modern science fiction in China.[2] Nathaniel Isaacson, a leading scholar of Chinese SF, gives priority of influence to Lu Xun, however, and regards him as critical in shaping the character of subsequent science fiction in the late 20th and early 21st centuries. For Isaacson it is Lu Xun's early essays, which he says are "haunted by the specter of an evanescent utopian past, a neo-Confucian vision of evolution as a process of social decline that could not be reversed," that helped him see that the "development of European science, literature, and culture in evolutionary terms, contrasted with China's inevitable decline" (57-58).[3] Like other post-May Fourth reformist intellectuals, Lu Xun's optimism about SF rested on a belief in "Mr. Science" as an antidote to that "evanescent utopian past" of the Confucian anti-modernists.[4] However, in some regards Lu Xun was also a deeply pessimistic thinker, one influenced by the work of Friedrich Nietzsche and Russian literature and still skeptical of humanist reason, as illustrated in his famous parable of an "iron house without windows or doors, utterly indestructible, and full of sound sleepers—all about to suffocate to death. Let them die in their sleep, and they will feel nothing. Is it right to cry out, to rouse the light sleepers among them, causing them inconsolable agony before they die?"[5] The metaphoric essence of this ultimately anti-humanist question repeats throughout many, if not all, of Lu Xun's writings, and he frequently offers only a negative answer—e.g., in stories of social cannibalism such as "A Madman's Diary," "In a Wineshop," and "Medicine," in which we are given glimpses into a society fraught with superstition, madness, misogyny, and a stultifying Confucian traditionalism.

Since the end of the Cultural Revolution in 1976 we

have frequently seen the literary influence of this more pessimistic, anti-humanist Lu Xun of madmen, corruption, and cannibalism. It manifested itself in the nativist "Roots-seeking fiction" (xungen wenxue) of the 1980s, and then again in the so-called "Hoodlum literature" (liumang wenxue) of the 1990s, but nowhere has it been quite so apparent as in the work of science fiction author Han Song. A full-time journalist for Xinhua News Agency, Han is considered one of China's three most prominent science fiction authors (along with Liu Cixin and Wang Jinkang), but his self-consciously weird writing style is distinct from his peers in its disregard for "hard science" in favor of a focus on the darker, aberrant consequences of China's modernization and technology-driven development. This darkness is something Chinese critics have frequently called attention to, pointing to Han's "gloomy vision" of the post-global world and its bizarre, eerie, indeterminate contours, or emphasizing how his grim vision of cosmic decline reflects what must be a Buddhistic (or nihilist) view of history.[6] In works such as *2066: Red Star Over America*, *Red Sea*, his recent *Hospital* trilogy, *High Speed Rail*, *Subway*, and novellas like "My Fatherland Does Not Dream," "The Passengers and the Creator," and "The Regenerated Bricks," Han does indeed imagine a hyper-technologized modernity that is both Western and inimical to Chinese culture. Thus in most of Han Song's work we can find the influence of the ambivalent Lu Xun, and as David Der-wei Wang points out in a compelling essay on the authors' inter-relationship, "literature in Han Song's mind is no longer able to directly refer to the original conditions of life imagined by the young Lu Xun, but [rather refers to] constant self-reference and deconstruction of 'primordial' (yuan) literature," which is strangely reminiscent of Lu Xun's "Mara poet," whose "malevolent voice is capable of upsetting and gnawing at people's hearts" (Wang 51).[7] In what follows I contend that Han gives "malevolent voice" to the contradictions of the present era by intentionally playing on his readers' "weird" anxieties and ethnocentric fears about China's experience of modernity and its rapid transformation under global capitalism.

To make this argument I will examine three of Han's most representative novellas with the assumption that they can best be studied comparatively, or from "the outside"—i.e., in terms of both their affinities with the wider Weird Fiction tradition and a psychological fixation with a racial "other" imagined as the West. If we are to believe the arrival of modernity initiates a crisis of representation, then the coming of a globalized "late modernity" exacerbates it, even to the point of producing, in Han's case, a surreal, psychically jarring mode of writing that depicts capitalist scientific and technological advances as productive of ever more terrifying and "sublimely weird" conditions. Han acknowledges this himself in an essay titled "Chinese Science Fiction as a Response to Modernization," wherein he argues that Western science and technology (and presumably modernity itself) "are like alien entities. If we [Chinese] buy into them, we turn ourselves into monsters, and that is the only way we can get along with Western notions of progress" (20). While such a statement borders on the xenophobic and seems strange coming from a science fiction author, it is not altogether unique. Benjamin Noys and Timothy Murphy distinguish between an Old Weird fiction (fl. 1890-1940) that hinges on reactionary politics, xenophobia toward immigrants, and "cosmic pessimism" toward science on the one hand, and an emergent New Weird that embraces the strangeness of new worlds, otherness, and alternate "ways of being" on the other (Noys and Murphy, 122). The Old Weird, mainly represented by H.P. Lovecraft's circle (Robert E. Howard, Seabury Quinn, and Clark Ashton Smith), famously "translates the avant-garde forms of modernity—futurism and the mathematical advances of non-Euclidean geometry underlying relativity theory—into objects of horror" and is more interested in science as a source of potential disaster (121). In contrast, the contemporary New Weird, as represented by writers like China Miéville and Jeff VanderMeer, tends to "prefer wonder to horror," claim Noys and Murphy, but they also acknowledge that some of these second generation Weird authors (e.g., Laird Barron and Thomas Ligotti) still conceive it as a "celebration of chaos and the logic of nihilism" (127).

Han, whose anti-modernity and emphasis on social chaos borders on the nihilistic, seems to share features with both generations of Weird writing. His fetishized images of China's "Others" (usually Caucasians/Westerners), even if we read them as a negative reaction to the cosmopolitan and supposedly multicultural values of global capitalism, are painfully reminiscent of the Old Weird authors in Lovecraft's circle. In another sense, foreigners represent for Han what Mark Fisher calls the weird's "sense of wrongness," or "a signal that the concepts and frameworks which we have previously employed are now obsolete" (13). Disruptively new, the psychological experience of weird writing appears as a supersession of "realism" that is not, as Fisher points out, "simply unpleasant either: there is an enjoyment in seeing the familiar in the conventional becoming outmoded—and enjoyment which, in its mixture of pleasure and pain, has something in common with what Lacan called *jouissance*" (ibid). Han's writing fits this description all too well, I contend, and his ethnocentric, racial phobias about the unfamiliar "foreigners" can even be understood in terms of Slavoj Zizek's "theft of enjoyment" thesis. According to this interpretation, racism and ethnocentrism are explained as a pleasurable fear of the Other (the immigrant or foreigner) who comes to take away our jobs, women, and resources—that is, our enjoyment or *jouissance*. As Zizek puts it,

> [w]hat is at stake in ethnic tensions is always [a kind of] possession: the 'other' wants to steal our enjoyment (by ruining our 'way of life') and/or he has access to some secret, perverse enjoyment. In short, what gets on our nerves, what really bothers us about the 'other' is the peculiar way he organizes his enjoyment (the smell of his food, his 'noisy' songs and dances, his strange manners, his attitudes to work—in the racist perspective, the 'other' is either a workaholic stealing our jobs or an idler living on our labour)." (Qtd in Hook, 42)

This explains why, in the final philosophical analysis, the sublimely weird experiences of Han's fiction invariably culminate in the discovery of a *lost* "sublime object" that causes the population to sink into a condition of abject degeneration. Thus, the cannibals of "The Passengers and the Creator" have literally had their native land stolen out from under them; in "My Fatherland Does Not Dream" the Chinese people have had their sleep stolen with drugs; and the foreign capitalists and scientists of "Regenerated Bricks" have even expropriated the restless souls of Chinese disaster-victims.

Han's (and our sympathetic reader's) pleasure in these kinds of dark nationalist fantasies is precisely located in a desire for the strange that is sustained by a displeasure in the (foreign) Other's enjoyment. In short, it is sublimely weird in the sense that this feeling is analogous to a *jouissance* which is "beyond the pleasure principle," and "a paradoxical pleasure procured by displeasure" (1989, 229). Moreover, produced in sharp contrast to China's older, officially sanctioned and responsibly aware "Socialist Realism," Han's work flouts linear plots and predictable types with a writing style that seems subversive. Thus, in terms of both psychological content and literary form, Han's surreal and "weirdly sublime" worlds depict a China that is constantly being undercut by technological and scientific "advances" that lead to ever more alien and yet perversely enjoyable conditions.[8]

The Sublime Abject of Technology

Imagine a man who can't remember his own name sitting forever on an airplane with a half-decayed corpse in the seat next to him. Here you have the basic setting of one of Han's most disturbingly typical stories, "The Passengers and the Creator." Such scenes are one reason science fiction critic Li Guanyi says that "no phrase captures Han Song's writing better than 'eerie' (*guiyi*). And in Han Song's eeriness, the most apparent characteristic is its indeterminacy. The majority of Han Song's stories feature one or more mysterious images, and often his stories offer no explanation at all regarding them" (29).[9] Li's observation calls to mind Mark Fisher's claim that in the late capitalist world the "eerie is fundamentally tied up with questions of agency" where actions and values seem increasingly spectral and "conjured out of nothing," and a world where "capital nevertheless exerts more influence than any allegedly substantial entity" (Fisher 14-15). Emerging from the indeterminate shadow of "Market" realities, Han's primal scenes and bizarre spectacles are frequently the product of a spectral capitalist technological development and strange economic conditions. Anyone who has read "The Passengers" will surely attest to such an eeriness: the plot is uncomplicated but memorably hinges on an eerie sense of missing agency in which, trapped onboard an unpiloted Boeing 747 that ceaselessly circles the planet, a few hundred amnesiac passengers survive on economy-class cannibalism. Since almost no one can remember a thing about their past lives, the passengers all accept that they were all born on the "7x7" and have no notion of the world outside the plane. Believing that they have no choice but to follow the plane's pre-established rules and routines of strict segregation into Economy, Business, and First classes, the docile inhabitants remain in their seats and survive on a mysterious soup until their health gradually deteriorates and they finally die. At some point the neighbor of the story's narrator, who later identifies himself by the name *Something*, takes him to see the dark underbelly of the plane where, deep down in the cargo compartment, he discovers the cannibalistic origins of the soup that nourishes all the passengers. Later, when *Something* shows the narrator an ID with the latter's picture on it, he discovers that he is the former captain of the 7x7—but shortly thereafter a coup led by the former co-pilot breaks out and *Something* is killed. Left alone, our awakened but trapped and terrified narrator finally jumps out of the 7X7 with a parachute made of life-jackets, whereupon he hears "a thundering roar, an unrestrained, unfiltered rumbling that sounds as if the universe were about to be turned on its head. Five thousand, maybe a hundred thousand 7x7 Worlds are flying above me. I turn my head up and suddenly see millions of shimmering windows, like pearls scattered in a dazzling array across the vault of heaven" (309-10). This terrible, irrational vision of hundreds of thousands of Boeing-made "aircraft-worlds" flooding the sky with cannibals represents a weirdly "sublime," agentless vision of the future.

As critics we are most accustomed to think of the sublime in Immanuel Kant's terms as the disjunctive experience of overwhelming scales, magnitudes too great to comprehend, or as some rupture in our understanding of time and space. For example, Kant describes how, on seeing St. Peter's in Rome, one has "a feeling of the inadequacy of his imagination for presenting the ideas of a whole, in which the imagination reaches its maximum and, in the effort to extend it, sinks back into itself" (*Critique* 83). The Kantian sublime has its primary representation in Nature, however, since only there does the sublime achieve an "intuition of the idea of infinity" (86). Most important for our purposes, he aligns the sublime against the beautiful as a peculiar kind of pleasure-in-pain, for "the feeling of the sublime is... at once a feeling of displeasure, arising from the inadequacy of imagination in the aesthetic estimation of magnitude to attain to its estimation by reason, and a simultaneously awakened pleasure, arising from this very judgement of the inadequacy of the greatest faculty of sense being in accord with ideas of reason, so far as the effort to attain to these is for us a law" (88). The experience of the sublime, then, is similar to Lacan's *jouissance* insofar as it too involves "the paradox of an object which, in the very field of representation, provides a view, in a negative way, of the dimension of the unrepresentable" (Zizek 230). The reason we experience such sublime displeasure is that a vast panorama of suffering and humiliation beyond representation opens up and, at the same time, achieves a negative representation in the stories of distinct objects or Things (American planes, commercial drugs, spirit bricks) which we are asked to contemplate as if from some outside, ethnic Other's infinite capacity for perversity—i.e., an unknown people without any comprehensible end or purpose.

The paradoxically alien, colossal qualities of unbridled human technological innovation have always been a key aspect of science fiction, traceable to the late-19th obsession with modern man's perverse scientific creativity (e.g., Dr. Frankenstein's). Indeed, Luddites and technophobes have ever since contended that the alienating, self-othering dimension of capitalist technology has had adverse consequences for the human spirit, and Han himself has claimed that science and technology are "foreign" entities, "not characteristic of Chinese culture" (*SFS* 2013, 20). Thus, critics such as Song Mingwei have gone so far as to describe "Passengers" as a tale about "the epic exile of the entire population of China to the air—their nation turned into a consumer society that has lost sovereignty to foreign manipulation" (*SFS* 2015, 91). Song further claims that the novella can be read as "a national allegory expressing profound anxiety about China's future," and this partly jibes with Han's own description of the story, which he has said is about how "humanity finds itself in an increasingly dark and despairing environment, with no way out of the endless and pervasive darkness" (SFS 2013, 20). "The Passengers and the Creator" is most definitely about the "darkness" and anxieties of Chinese modernity, particularly its "abject" qualities, as can be seen in its apocalyptic ending, when the captain, dazed and confused at the plane crash site, spies "a group of metal carapaces like cockroaches riding on four wheels speeding toward me. [...] From inside the metal carapaces, a number of golden haired, tin white-skinned men leap out, speaking in a garbled tongue I cannot understand. Is it 'them'?" ("Passenger," 312).[10] Presumably these Caucasians have taken over the planet and exiled the remaining Chinese to the air in Boeing's infernal planes, but this is nowhere directly stated in this very odd story.

Critic Li Guanyi observes that "besides reflecting contemporary Chinese social reality in his work," several of Han's short stories and novellas reveal "China as 'self' [ziwo] and America always as 'other' [tazhe]. These works reflect a common mentality among today's Chinese educated youth: not only do they feel dissatisfied with today's society's problems, they point to America as the [main] Western country that uses these problems to 'contain China'" (Li 106). Han's method of deflecting criticism away from China and onto the US is important to understand, especially in the context of the abovementioned problem of the (Western) Old Weird's transparent ethnocentrism, its anti-immigrant anxiety, and racist discourse. That is, here again there appears to be a connection between writing the weird and xenophobia or ethnic anxiety, and indeed some Lovecraft critics have aligned this tendency with what the psychoanalytic philosopher Julia Kristeva calls the "abject," or a kind of psychological "frontier," or "repulsive gift that the Other, having become alter ego, drops so that 'I' does not disappear in it but finds, in that sublime alienation, a forfeited existence" (Kristeva 236).[11] This abject psychological terrain, where one comes to realize the Other in oneself, produces a moment of "sublime alienation" in section 23, when the narrator ejects himself from the air plane:

> A red orb, shimmering all over, emerges unsteadily from the depths of what must be the Light, and soon it has become so bright that I can no longer look directly at it. In that instant, I hear the arrow of time shoot past my ear with a whirr. Ashamed, I lower my head and see a pile of broken human bodies emerging from the water-stained shimmer. The passengers who jumped with me are still wearing their orange parachutes [...] And *Something*—did he ever really exist, or will he ever exist? And once we had broken free of the fetters of speed and course, only our World would descend and fall to the ground. What about the tens of millions other Worlds? And what about my fellow men who go on flying through the darkness? (310-11)

The narrator's dejected feelings of awe, shame, and uncertainty are coupled with his loss of identity and world, and here prompt a moment of Lovecraftian verbal excess— an outflowing of words that cannot quite "add up" to, or "capture," the feelings and phenomena being described.[12]

This outflowing of verbal excess, one senses, is also what cannot be adequately contained, a flow of speech that cannot be held back by an "other."

According to Chinese SF author and critic Jia Liyuan (who writes SF under the pen-name Fei Dao), Han's "'Gloomy China,' with its veiled elements of political protest, amounts to what Fredric Jameson termed a 'national allegory'" (Jia 110). That is, in Jameson's well-known "Third World Allegory" thesis, one could easily read stories like "The Passengers" as a re-telling of the nation's modernization narrative, but "at the same time its strong philosophical and even religious flavor transcends concerns with the nation-state to become a universal exploration of the meaning of human existence" (Jia 110).[13] However, Jameson's claim is that developing nations like China tend to construct self-consciously allegorical tales that represent the collectivity relying on local "types" acting out characteristic relationships. His primary example is Lu Xun's "The True Story of Ah-Q" (*Ah-Q zheng chuan*), about a village idiot with a persecution complex who ultimately becomes a convenient scapegoat and is executed as a revolutionary.[14] According to Jameson this kind of work is "qualitatively different" from Western fiction because it depicts "a social and a historical nightmare, a vision of the horror of life specifically through History itself, whose consequences go far beyond the more local western realistic or naturalistic representation" (Jameson 1986, 71). By this logic, the forgetful ghouls trapped on board these American planes are suggestive of some real, widespread historical nightmare condition that Han wants his readers to become aware of.

While it is no longer a Third World country, China

has historically been abused, contained, and colonized by foreign countries (particularly England and Japan): it rightly looks with suspicion at the outside world. On this account it is important to take into consideration Frank Dikötter's work on China's rhetoric of "national humiliation," wherein "public admission of national weakness and sensitivity are considered to be clear proof of the nation's own moral superiority. Feelings of self-deprecation, complaints about an exaggerated sensitivity and a sense of internal vengefulness have characterized [modern Chinese] cultural nationalism" (600). If we read Han's novella as an "allegory of national containment"— that is, as an allegory of the United States' attempt to constrain or contain China's global ambitions—we can easily see how those American-made planes, airborne prisons really, are not just representatives of a world that runs on ubiquitous US technology, but the "Thing" (or *objet petit a*) that generates a a sublime sense of "self-deprecation." I will discuss this allegorical aspect further in the conclusion, but first another tour through one of Han's future hells is in order.

The Nightmare of History

Han's most important novella, "My Fatherland Does Not Dream" (*Wode zuguo bu zuo meng*, ca. 2007), is a work that has been discreetly forgotten—i.e., it cannot be found in any of his published anthologies and, according to my research, is only available as a samizdat version that still circulates on the internet.[15] The reason for this is, no doubt, the sensitive nature of the topic that the story focuses on: the official use of narcotics to exploit laborers in a near-future China. Writing just prior to the notorious spate of suicides at Foxconn factories in southern China (suicides brought on by overwork, with employees being forced to work overtime 17-20 hours a day), Han addresses the problem of capitalist exploitation in an original way.[16] The protagonist of the story, Xiao Ji, is a fatigued young man who wakes up exhausted every morning and tries to contend with his failing marriage. Visiting a pub one night he meets a strange American who speaks good Chinese and is referred to only as "the foreigner" (*waiguo ren*) throughout the story. This foreigner offers to explain the source of his woes: if Xiao Ji can avoid taking the drug called Defatigue™ (*qu kunling*) and stay awake for one night, the secret of his exhaustion will be revealed. As it turns out, the reason Xiao Ji has been feeling fatigued is that his (and everyone else's) body is exhausted from working both day and night, as the drug puts one in a docile, zombie-like state that they are nevertheless able to work in:

> "What are they doing?" Xiao Ji asked fearfully. "Ah, them, the spirits [linghun] of the night," the foreigner mysteriously replied, pointing to the group of weird people. Soon it was discovered that they had been assigned the important job of dealing with dangerous elements and aliens in society: heavy metal rock singers, pioneer novelists, political pop artists, and X generation directors. Underground religious activists, Falun Gong addicts, national separatist forces, Taiwan independence elements. Of course, the dangerous elements themselves are also in a state of sleepwalking. As soon as they were discovered by the Red Armband Brigade, they were turned around and sent to a place with few people:

incineration in the boiler room of the enterprise, or directly corroded by sulfuric acid. (Trans. mine, Han 10)[17]

Here we have a striking glimpse of weird "wrongness," but one in which a repressed historical guilt (the Red Brigades of the Cultural Revolution) has returned to the surface to haunt the present. Ironically, in a deep trance, the workers and malcontents are unable to puncture this "surface" and emerge into actual social reality.

The story's *Inferno*-like vision of China reflects on today's neoliberal reality and amplifies the ways in which it capitalizes, via a brutally efficient biopolitical regime, on both the waking and "dreaming" lives of the people. Such a dark, vast image of exploitation returns us to the issue of the sublime object or Thing that baffles and confuses. However, in Han's story it is not precisely the regime responsible for drugging the population that he is concerned with, but the "weirding" effect it has on the reader. Eugene Thacker has drawn attention to how, in Kant's idea of the sublime, there is always already some object or thing, "even [one] devoid of form, so far as it immediately involves, or else by its presence provokes, a representation of limitlessness" (qtd in Thacker 116). Such representations of limitlessness, however, inspire an "aesthetic relation to something that is, strangely, nothing"—which is to say, the point is not the sublime thing per se, but the outcome or experience of it that matters. The only consolation then is that, even if we cannot comprehend this object, "we can, at the very least, comprehend this incomprehension – we can think the failure of thought" (117). This paradoxical formulation of the sublime is quite suited to Han Song's work, I believe, for atop simple conspiracy plots his stylistic talents are usually devoted to describing such a "failure of thought"— for example, in the "The Passengers and the Creator," the unwitting voyagers are in Kristeva's state of "abject alienation," or a fixed relation to an unknown "Creator" (the Western Other) of an airborne hell. Similarly, in Xiao Ji's bewildered reaction to hundreds of millions of docile sleepwalkers going to work and shopping, there is an awesome sense of agentless purpose (hastily attributed to whatever shadowy forces the Foreigner is working for)— that is, until he discovers that Party Officials are responsible for the worker-narcotics.

Han's sublimely weird vision of China is not just a defamiliarizing technique, then, but also his work's chief psychological element. That is, one of the most characteristic motifs of his eerie world is its paranoid fixation on the alien, outlandish, foreign Other. In "My Fatherland" he offers his most direct version of this, depicting Xiao Ji and "the Foreigner" in a relationship that shifts from uncomfortable, to hostile, to abject. We see these shifts, for example, when the Foreigner reveals that Xiao Ji's wife is having an affair with an older man:

> Xiao Ji cried with sadness. What made him feel even more humiliated was that the scene of his wife's disgrace was first discovered by a foreigner. He felt ashamed about *how the shame of the Chinese is always shown to foreigners no matter what. Maybe, he was deliberately showing it to Xiao Ji. Behind the cheerful outward appearance of foreigners there are hidden traces of a dirty psychology.* Here, he wants to beat the hell out of this guy and vent all

> the anger he can't vent on others these days. But in the end, he just thought it over and didn't dare do it. After all, he's a foreigner, and besides, no matter what his aim was, he still let Xiaoji know his wife's big secret. (Trans. and italics mine, 11) [18]

If this peculiarly xenophobic passage reveals a deep mistrust and tortured anxiety toward the ethnic other, it also trades on stock images of foreigners as inscrutable types who harbor ill will behind a cheerful façade. Xiao Ji's initial reaction to his cuckolding is humiliation both for himself and, somehow, for his nation—but this turns quickly into an anger that dies out as fast it flares up. This conflict between an infiltrating foreigner and a "shamed" Chinese worker would appear to substantiate Jia's claim that Han is working primarily as an allegorist, but there is something far more elaborate at work in this story.

Later in the story Xiao Ji, armed, desperate, and on the run from the secret police, returns to the hotel where his wife and the older man have their night-time trysts. Breaking into their room he discovers that the other man is not only fully awake but an important member of a secret government committee responsible for the drugging and overwork. In his long explanation, "delivered like a speech at a party congress," the VIP tells Xiao Ji, "We are facing a dangerous international and domestic environment. In this turbulent and perilous world, Chinese people cannot dream [...] Now, China poses a real threat to them [the US]. Sleepwalking has awakened 1.3 billion Chinese people. Although reform and opening up have been going on for this many years, China in the daytime, when we look at it seriously, is often just a plate of scattered sand. But a truly powerful China has now appeared at night" (23). The official's rationalization of the use of drugs and dreamlessness reveals what could be considered the "limitless wrongness" of the situation, especially because it appears to persuade even Xiao Ji that what the regime is doing is somehow reasonable. His patriotic desire to support his country apparently overrides his desire to resist, insinuated by the Foreigner we are to understand, and finally also his desire to "dream" within China. One can only account for this conversion, I think, by assuming that he finally becomes one of Kristeva's abject "devisers of territories," a person so dejected he "never stops demarcating his universe, whose fluid confines— for they are constituted by a non-object, the abject—constantly question his solidity and impel him to start afresh" (Kristeva 67). Like the narrator of "The Passengers," Xiao Ji loses both his society and his identity and is thereby plunged into an abyss of alienation that he tries to recuperate on the "outside" (abroad) among the foreigners he is suspicious of but must face up to.

Thus while the point of departure for many works of Old Weird fiction is some deep-seated ethnic anxiety, or a sense of "alien wrongness," in Han's stories we see a similar fixation with the foreign. In Lovecraft's "The Horror at Red Hook," it is the devil-worshipping émigrés in tunnels beneath New York, while in "The Shadow Over Innsmouth," the New England antiquarian narrator finds himself trapped in a village occupied by "degenerate" fish-folk, human troglodytes with foreign blood who, it turns out, are actually his kinfolk. By contrast, Han's protagonists never discover their "inner alien," and there is often disturbing ethnic anxiety toward the *waiguo ren* who fuels clandestine plots and gives his stories a distinctly exotic flavor. Still, if my "Fatherland Does Not Dream" is an allegory of China's modern, biopolitical state, with its zombie-like masses playing the role of the political unconscious, it follows that the Party VIP's literal, unironic claim that the "Chinese people cannot afford dream" is a direct criticism of the people in charge. However, the story seems to roll that conclusion back by inserting the role of the Foreigner, a kind of Ghost of Christmas Future, who presents Xiao Ji with a corrupt, "dirty" vision of the consequences of China's wholesale adoption of technocratic capitalism. So the Other can be useful, can offer us a clearer vision of ourselves, it is a vision we will probably step away from. In short, we wind up back at Lu Xun's parable of the "iron house": waking up the masses will only exacerbate their suffering, and the Foreigner who tempts the Chinese with a chance to reclaim their agency is doubted, loathed, and finally dismissed from the story. And yet, at the end of the story Xiao Ji turns away from the task of awakening society, takes his (still dreaming) wife and goes in search of "a place where people can still dream." In this highly disturbing novella Han Song explicitly evokes a sense of weird sublimity, daring to "think the failure of thought" in his society, by depicting China as a vast zombie-driven workforce, slaving away for consumer goods both day and night. However, he finally suggests that the desire to enlighten or "awaken" others is untenable, a modern idea that falters on the reality of people who "cannot afford to dream" in their attempt to catch up with the West.

132 • Ron Judy

Dreams of Ruin

The novella "Regenerated Bricks," Han's story about the traumatic aftermath of the Wenchuan Earthquake of 2008, in which 87,587 people died, is a brilliant, far more sophisticated work of weird fiction. In it, an architect has discovered how to trap the spirits of the dead within bricks made from the debris of Sichuan's devastated areas. When they go into production supernatural phenomena occur, and these inhabit the structures that are built from them. The "regenerated bricks" (*zaisheng*, lit. rebirth), described as profoundly beautiful in their simplicity, are first exhibited in Europe, where they begin to gain popularity abroad as works of art. It is only later that their ability to emit light and strange music is discovered, and then eventually they demonstrate the supernatural power to reveal quantum reality through the songs of those souls. The narrator of this story is, again, a somewhat weak, bewildered young man who is attempting (circa the 2030s) to piece together the broken genealogy of his family from the earthquake's ruins. Like Xiao Ji, his attempts to identify himself, gain agency, and give his family a narrative end in failure because the discourse of the regenerated spirit-bricks depicts it as a great scientific triumph.

The science fiction author and scholar Wang Yao (a.k.a., Xia Jia) has observed that all these darker, more macabre elements in Han Song's writing suggests that "all that appears to be a hopeful liberation or a road to escape or redemption is nothing more than the achievement of a benighted, samsaric fate the main characters are sealed within" (Wang 27).[19] Han's work is indeed sometimes very claustrophobic, and perhaps this does reveal a kind of Buddhist fatalism insofar as his characters are trapped within fundamentally unfree futures, but this element of his writing also coincides with the origins of the English "weird" in the *wyrd,* Old English for "fate".

It is easy to conflate fate with fatalism, however, and it's the latter that is more apparent when reading Han Song, especially given the apocalyptic nature of this story and the mode of its response to an historic natural disaster.

The *zaisheng zhuan,* "rebirth bricks," are able to access the energy of the dead, even though everyone seems to believe the process brings them back to life. As the narrator very colorfully puts it:

> [B]ased on the architect's instruction, the shattered tiles and bricks still contained the feelings that had been invested in them previously. Although it was discarded building materials that had been "regenerated" (*zaisheng*) materially, it was also a "regeneration" built on the spiritual and emotional plane following the catastrophe. When the architect said such things, he all but closed his eyes, like a preacher reciting scripture in church, which imparted a warmth akin to a spring breeze blowing in one's face [...] This is of course my perception as a latecomer, so perhaps there is a generation gap involved. (18-19)

Slowly recounting all the historic discoveries up to his own time in the future (and after it is discovered that the bricks are able to reveal the inner workings of the cosmos), the narrator reveals that the architect was his father and it is his goal is to recount the history of the bricks. Here we can see a "weird" Chinese emphasis on social duty and moral obligations to the parents, one that reflects well on the protagonist-hero's aim of doing good by his clan. More importantly, the story is a commentary on Chinese ancestor-worship and the way a culture reveres the dead, and how that custom fits into modernity.[20]

The historical, genealogical significance of the bricks (as 're-generational') is put into question by the above musings about their creator/discoverer, the architect (who is likely our narrator's father). One way to understand these artifacts would be via Walter Benjamin's notion of the aura, as discussed in "The Work of Art in the Age of Mechanical Reproduction": the power clinging to primitive, premodern, and pre-industrial art. In contrast to the sterility of dead, empty works of mass-produced art, he describes this aura as a "strange tissue of space and time: the unique apparition of a distance, however near it may be. To follow with the eye—while resting on a summer afternoon—a mountain range on the horizon or a branch that casts its shadow on the beholder is to breathe the aura of those mountains, of that branch" (Benjamin 23). The "aura" of the regenerated bricks lies in their material and spiritual capacity to contain the memories of the victims of the 2008 Wenchuan Earthquake, literally as "apparitions" that retain the nature and essence of the not-so-distant past. However, in the end, it is perhaps better to identify them in terms of an "abject aura":

> Later on a British scientist discovered regenerated atoms, which he considered to be basic particles of matter, and whoever grasped this would be able to avoid free energy reverting to zero and thus would never reach absolute entropy. . . Once it was realized that the universe was very possibly a ruin that could be described using quantum

matrix mechanics, people were able to set their minds at rest, believing that this resource could be used for hundreds of millions of years. (40)

Here we finally discover the bricks' power of *zaisheng*, "rebirth," which, in never reaching absolute entropy, remain forever in a state of disorderly ruin—traumatic and yet full of negative potential. Ironically the humans can "put their minds at rest" in the knowledge that their vampiric exploitation of the afterlife can go on, on a ruined planet, not in defiance of entropy, but in the peaceful awareness that the heat death of the universe will never affect them or their immediate descendants.

Eventually the narrative reveals that the science behind *zaisheng*-matter itself is driven by profits and mankind's vampiric relation to the world, so that at one level the story allegorizes the corporate and official corruption revealed in the wake of the Wenchuan Earthquake. Thus the restless spirits of the earthquake victims are eventually commodified, even "mechanized," and sold on the market: "On earth, people began to use regenerated brick to build another Tower of Babel...As for the material for the main structure, it was brought from southwestern China [Sichuan], so a major transportation artery was constructed from China to the Middle East, which was called the new Silk Road of the ruins" (34). With bitter irony, Han places the aftermath of the 2008 earthquake in perspective as an unsentimental, anti-modern tale of our descent into a tomorrow where continued profiteering exploits all matter, no matter how sacred or precious. Allegorically at least, the bricks are revealed, in all their auratic wrongness, to be figures for a kind of capitalist imagination in all its timeless, cosmic horror—that is, as an imagination that thrives on a "sublime alienation/abjection" that both disrupts time and space and reveals our dislocation from our own (in this case, Chinese) history.

David Der-wei Wang explains this dislocation in his *The Monster That is History*, pointing out that Chinese modernity has been experienced as an "attempt to grapple with a polymorphous reality" sparked by the intrusion of the West, a reality that was felt to be alien and yet desirable. Wang writes of the necessity of confronting the "monstrous fact of contested modernities" and, turning on its side Fredric Jameson's famous pronouncement that "History is what hurts," claims that as far as modern Chinese literature is concerned, "History is that which haunts" (Wang 12). In the way of WWII, the Great Famine, and the Cultural Revolution, a "ghostly narrative leads us to the task of memory and mourning. Across corporeal and temporal-spatial barriers, ghosts reappear like vanishing memories and perished relations, while they 'embody' the hiatus between the dead and the living, the unreal and the real, the unthinkable and the admissible" (ibid). Wang's haunted history of modern Chinese culture is liminal, a both/and condition that deconstructs thinking about the present, but in my view it does not give enough weight to the tremendous psychological impact of China's integration into the global order, or the ways in which its ghostly narratives are frequently recollected as traumatic defeats or psychic wounds that sustain nationalist narratives. Hence, in describing Han's weird historical novella I have tried to emphasize how it depicts a kind of cosmic fatalism and the bizarre outcomes associated with

China's global capitalist development and (post)modernity. For example, the work turns against Chinese modernity by reflecting on the ways in which ancestor-worship has been trivialized to the point of an absurdity; and it also criticizes the ways in which China's Silk Road heritage is revived as a gimmick.

Finally, unfolding in a certain abject outflowing of "verbal excess," the story culminates in the incomprehensible situation of a ruined Sichuan—that famously eerie part of China's southwest periphery—where even the dead can know no peace. That is, like "My Fatherland Does not Dream," here we also see a depiction of the masses (of the dead) who are subjected to eternal restlessness. Thus, we can perhaps agree, as both Li and Fisher contend, that the weird and/or eerie signals a deep uncertainty about the present as well as an unsettling anxiety about the Other, only here with the added Chinese sense of *guiyi*, or "aberrant otherness." The sublime object of Han's "Regenerated Bricks" is the *guiyi* ancestors within the bricks who have been commodified by a neoliberal science that constantly tries to harness and subjugate; dead ancestors that are also a reminder of the present's failure to honor the past. Whichever way we read it, the story's weird historicism (and its fatalistic reading of China's future) is remarkable for its haunting descriptions of the "hiatus between the unthinkable and admissible."

Conclusions: the Sublime Object(s) of Chinese Modernity

Resurrecting the spirit of Lu Xun's Mara poets who mercilessly unveil society's terrible truths, Han Song reimagines modernism as a disturbing, sublimely weird experience of otherness. Breaking with Socialist Realism and dedication to positive images of China's development history, Han conceives a far more pessimistic cultural landscape—one that places no hope in Mr. Science, relies on a weird and sometimes grotesque writing style, and taps into the discourse of Chinese national humiliation to imagine his people in various stages of abjection. Han's tales are thus parables of the disaster of global integration and multi-culturalism on a grand scale: the Chinese Passengers inside that unlikely symbol of American technological supremacy (the Boeing 7x7) are subject to a mysterious Creator, figuratively consuming one another, while locked inside an "alien" symbol of modernity that transports them nowhere. Thus, while these works all directly and paranoically suggest that China is everywhere vulnerable to outside forces eager to take over or subvert her, they also imagine that no matter how she adapts to the Westernized world of globalization the Chinese people will eventually "turn themselves into monsters," as Han puts it in his essay.

As I argued at the beginning of this essay, the sublime weirdness of Han's work resides in its focus on the "theft of enjoyment" theme, i.e., inscriptions of an "object" that is overladen with a pathos that is pleasurably painful (fearful) to imagine or, Jameson would say, to allegorize. As Derek Hook summarizes, we should remember that "forms of excess stimulation (the 'negative pleasure' of *jouissance*) underlie and propel Symbolic and political constructions of otherness. Different cultural modes of enjoyment are, furthermore, fundamentally discordant. We have then not so much a 'Clash of Civilizations'—to reference Samuel

Huntington's (1997) much cited thesis—as a clash of enjoyments" (Hook 37). Again, considering how "The Passengers" ends with a vision of wholesale imprisonment of the Chinese people by blonde-haired foreigners, "Regenerated Bricks" revolves around an image of Chinese spirit-entities being recycled and consumed in the global economy, and "My Fatherland Does Not Dream" dramatizes the humiliation of a foreigner witnessing the wholesale zombification of the Chinese people, we see a consistent pattern of connecting "excess stimulation" to experiences of national humiliation beneath the gaze of the Western other. Indeed, all three of Han's novellas begin and end in moments of excruciating national embarrassment or even humiliation—scenes rich in that abject feeling of "national horror" discussed above, wherein some aspect of China's identity *relative to* the West is taken over, undermined, or perverted. Despite a shrinkage in scope, this horror is parallel to Lovecraftian "cosmic horror" insofar as it deals with threatening beings "from beyond" (foreigners, ghosts) that are capable of conjuring up "weird" feelings of ethno-nationalism that can no longer be merely allegorized (vis-à-vis Lu Xun). It's imperative that we look critically at these features of Han's writing, not simply because they are similar to earlier Old Weird tendencies, but because they reveal underlying "structures of feeling" that Western audiences might relate to and care about.

Notes

[1] Quoted in Jia, p. 106.

2 However, *A Tale of the Moon Colony* (1905) by pseudonymous author Huangjiang Diaosou is considered the first Chinese science fiction novel.

3 "The History of Man" (*Ren zhi lishi*, 1907), "Lessons from the History of Science" (*Kexue shi jiao pian*, 1907), "On Uneven Cultural Development" (Wenhua pianzhi lun, 1907), "On the Power of Mara Poetry" (*Moluo shi li shuo*, 1907), and "Toward a Refutation of Malevolent Voices" (*Po'e sheng lun*, 1908).

4 The May Fourth Movement was a widespread, highly influential student protest incited by the unfair treatment of China at the Paris Peace Conference ending World War I in 1919. It was also a high point of the progressive New Culture Movement which called for the abolition of the patriarchal, Confucian social order, an end to classical learning, official use of vernacular writing (*bai hua wen*), and numerous other reforms. An excellent contemporary overview is Zhang Longxi's "Literary Modernity in Perspective," in *A Companion to Chinese Literature*, ed. Zhang Yingjin (New York: Blackwell, 2016): 41-53.

5 See, "Preface to *Call to Arms*," in *Selected Stories of Lu Hsun*, trans. Yang Hsien-yi and Gladys Yang (Peking: Foreign Languages Press, 1972) p. 24.

6 See Song Mingwei's introduction to *The Reincarnated Giant*: "[compared to Liu Cixin] Han Song's style is more provocative both artistically and politically. He is often compared to Kafka, but a more relevant comparison is no doubt Lu Xun. His sf writings are full of uncanny, gloomy, and sometimes inexplicable images that aim to unconceal reality's dark underbelly," p. XVII.

7 Wang's article is essential reading insofar it is the first assessment of Han's writing by a prominent international

critic; moreover, in naming Han Song the heir to the "Lu Xun legacy of thought about science and literature," p. 50.

[8] One of Han's most characteristic quirks, for example, is his repeated depictions of claustrophobic social spaces, especially advanced transportation systems—as can be seen from a glance at the titles of some of his works: the novels *Subway* (*ditie*) and *High Speed Rail* (*gaotie*), the stories "Submarines" (*qianting*), "Security Check" (*an jian*) and other works that deal with scenarios where large crowds experience great agitation and transformation.

[9] Here I'm referencing the page numbers of Nathaniel Isaacson's (partial) translation of Li's 2007 article, "Eerie Parables and Prophecies: an Analysis of Han Song's Science Fiction." (*Chinese Literature Today*, 7.1, 2018) 28-32. The third, missing section of the original, will be discussed below, p. 5.

[10] For unknown reasons the critic Song Mingwei mischaracterizes the ending of the story: "The passengers take over the plane and force it to land. As they disembark, they are confronted by armed US soldiers. In this future, China's rise has been eclipsed by American technology, consumerism, and military might," p 91. This is not what happens in the Chinese edition or the Nathaniel Isaacson translation, which is quoted here. I draw attention to this because it reveals how easily the urge to allegorize goes awry of close reading.

[11] For more on abject Weirdness, see David Simmons' "A Certain Resemblance": Abject Hybridity in H. P. Lovecraft's Short Fiction," in *New Critical Essays on H.P. Lovecraft* (New York: Palgrave, 2013): 13-30.

[12] China Miéville suggest that this "obsessive qualification and stalling of the noun" is a function of sublime

uncertainty in a "world is always-already unrepresentable, and can only be approached by an asymptotic succession of subjective pronouncements," p. 511-12.

[13] According to Chiara Cigarini, if the "process of modernization experienced by the count[r]y" is the point, as critics like Jia Liyuan claim, then "this process is connected with the recuperation of an aesthetic rooted in ancient Chinese literary tradition, aimed at expressing the importance of Chinese history as well as a global excessive reliance on technology," p. 251.

[14] It is worth considering Wang Qin's (2013) argument point that Jameson's use of the "national" is already a narrative category or form of writing in itself, one that operates as "a conceptual apparatus for a critique of multinational capitalism in terms of literature," p. 657.

[15] The edition I refer to here is available at https://journals.openedition.org/ideo/471file=1.
However, according to Zhihu at least two editions of the text exist(ed).

[16] See Ngai and Chan's "Global Capital, the State, and Chinese Workers: The Foxconn Experience" for a fuller account of working conditions at the factories, and the 14 suicides that took place there in 2010 alone.

[17] From p. 10, my translation.

[18] Thanks to the non-specificity of number in Chinese, the speaker could be referring to this particular foreigner, or "foreigners" in general.

[19] Sheldon Hsiao-peng Lu has written persuasively of how the late-Qing classical tale, which for him means the "Post-Strange Tales from a Chinese Study" (*Hou liaozhai zhiyi*) short fiction of Wang T'ao, had a very deep influence on modern Chinese authors like Lu Xun and Liang Qichao.

See esp., p. 749-50. Perhaps more pertinently, Lisa Raphals has suggested that "both late-Qing and contemporary new-wave science fiction draw on *zhiguai* fiction" (which dates back to the Six Dynasties Period, 220-589 CE) and its shared concern with how "strange" animal-human crossings and transformations. Both this medieval genre of strange tales and its latter-day equivalent in Wang T'ao, have definite echoes in Han Song's work, so it is important to research these further to determine how a native "Strange Tale" tradition interacts with the global socio-economic order through his work.

[20] According to the scholar of classical Chinese fiction Wang Ping, the marginal social role played by early fiction authors "produced a painful situation in which, on the one hand they hoped to realize a sense of self-value [ziwo jiazhi], and on the other a harsh [social] reality blocked all hope of that realization," and hence their work "intentionally reveals the darkness of officialdom, but also shows their class sense of social responsibility" (Wang 101-02). Wang's explanation of the officials' pessimistic attitudes is, I think, highly relevant to the work of Han Song—who is also a government official employed by the state-owned Xinhua News Agency.

Works Cited

Chen, Qiufan (陈楸帆). "Cultivating on the Edge of the Weird: An Interview with Renowned SF Author Han Song." [Guiyi bianyuan de xiuxingzhe: zhuming kehuan zuojia Han Song zhuanfang]. *World Science Fiction* [Shijie kehuan bolan], Sept. 2007: 13-14.

Chen, Shujie (陈舒劼). "The Challenge of the Other: the Monster Phenomenon in Chinese SF Since 1990" [Tazhe de tiaozhan:

1990 yilai zhongguo kehuan xiaoshuo de yaowu xianxiang]. *Modern Chinese Literature Studies* [Zhongguo xiandai wenxue yanjiu zongkan], November, 2020: 123-136.

Cigarini, Chiara. "Hearing Technological Anomalies: an Analysis of Han Song's 'The Rebirth Bricks'." *Frontiers in Literary Studies*, Vol. 14, #2 (2020): 228-253.

Dikötter, Frank. "Culture 'Race' and Nation: The Formation of National Identity in Twentieth Century China." *Journal of International Affairs*. Vol. 49, #2 (1996): 590-605.

Fisher, Mark. *The Weird and the Eerie*. London: Repeater Books, 2017.

Han, Song (韩松). "The Passengers and the Creator." Trans. Nathaniel Isaacson. *The Reincarnated Giant*. Ed. Theodore Huters, Song Mingwei, et al. New York: Columbia UP, 2019.

----. "Chengke yu chuangzao zhe." *Chengke yu chuangzao zhe: Han Song zhongduan pian kehuan xiaoshuo xuan*. (*The Passengers and the Creator: Selected Han Song Science Fiction Novellas*). HK: Hong Kong Open Page Publ., 2019.

----. "Regenerated Bricks." Trans. *The Reincarnated Giant*. Ed. Theodore Huters, Song Mingwei, et al. New York: Columbia UP, 2019.

----. "Chinese Science Fiction as a Response to Modernization." *Science Fiction Studies*, Vol. 40, No. 1 (March 2013): 15-21.

----. "Zaisheng zhuan." (Rebirth Bricks). *Wenyi fengshang* (Literary Trends). #1 (Dec. 2010): 59-71.

----. "Wode zuguo bu zuo meng." (My Fatherland Does not Dream). OpenEdition Journals, available at https://journals.openedition.org/ideo/471?file=1 Accessed 26 Oct. 2020.

----. "Science Fiction is the News of the Future." Author's personal blog, available at http://hansong.blog.caixin.com/archives/42027 Accessed 25 Oct. 2020.

Hook, Derek. "Pilfered Pleasure: on Racism as the 'Theft of Enjoyment,' in *Lacan and Race: Racism, Identity, and Psychoanalytic Theory*. Ed. Sheldon George and Derek Hook. New York: Routledge, 2022.

Isaacson, Nathaniel. *Celestial Empires: the Emergence of Chinese Science Fiction*. Middletown: Wesleyan UP, 2017.

Jia, Liyuan (賈立元, 飛氘). "Gloomy China: China's Image in Han Song's Science Fiction." Tr. Joel Martinsen. *Science Fiction Studies*, Vol. 40 (2013): 103-115.

Kant, Immanuel. *The Critique of Judgement*. Trans. James Creed Meredith. London: Oxford UP, 2007.

Kristeva, Julia. Kristeva, *Powers of Horror: An Essay on Abjection*. Trans. Leon S. Roudiez New York: Columbia University Press, 1982.

----. Kristeva, Julia. *The Julia Kristeva Reader*. New York: Columbia, 1997.

Li, Guangyi. (李广益). "Weirdness and Uncertainty—a Critique of Han Song's Science Fiction" [*Guiyi yu bu queding xing: dangdai zuojia pingxi*] *Modern Author Critiques*, #1 (2007): 102-106.

Liu, Zhirong (刘志荣). *Dangdai zhongguo kehuan Zhong de jige wenti*. (Some humanistic issues in Contemporary Chinese Science Fiction). *Southern Cultural Forum*. (2012): 51–58.

Lu, Hsiao-peng (Sheldon). "Waking to Modernity: The Classical Tale in Late-Qing China." *The New Literary History*. Vol. 34, #4 (2004): 745-760.

Luo, Trista. *Kehuan xiaoshuo jia Han Song: kehuan bushi xie naxie yuan zai tianbian de shi* (Science Fiction Author Han Song: SF is not About Those Remote, Marginal Things). *Orange News*, July 16, 2019. http://www.orangenews.hk/culture/system/2019/07/16/0 10121563.shtml Accessed 24 Oct. 2020.

Lu Xun. *Selected Stories of Lu Hsun*. Trans. Yang Hsien-yi and Gladys Yang. Peking: Foreign Languages Press, 1972.

Miéville, China. "Weird Fiction." In *The Routledge Companion to Science Fiction*, Ed. by Mark Bould. Oxford: Routledge, 2009: 510–17.

Murphy, Timothy S. "Supremely Monstrous Thought: H. P. Lovecraft and the Weirding of World Literature." *Genre*, vol. 49, #2 (2016): 159-79.

Ngai, Pun, and Jenny Chan. "Global Capital, the State, and Chinese Workers: The Foxconn Experience." *Modern China*, vol 38, #4 (2012): 383-410.

Noys, Benjamin & Timothy Murphy. "Introduction: Old and New Weird." *Genre*, vol. 49, #2 (2016): 117-134.

Nye, David E. Narratives and Spaces: Technology and the Construction of American Culture. New York: Columbia UP, 1997.

Raphals, Lisa. "Chinese Science Fiction and its Doubles." *Science Fiction and the Dismal Science: Essays on Economics in and of the Genre*. Eds. Westfahl & Benford. Jefferson: MacFarland, 2019.

Song, Ming-wei (宋明炜). "Variations on Utopia in Contemporary Chinese Science Fiction." *Science Fiction Studies*. Vol. 40, #1 (March 2013): 86-102.

----. "After 1989: The New Wave of Chinese Science Fiction." *China Perspectives*. 2015.1 (2015): 7-13.

Sorensen, Leif. "A Weird Modernist Archive: Pulp Fiction, Pseudobiblia, H. P. Lovecraft." *Modernism/modernity*, Vol. 17, #3 (September 2010): 501-522

Thacker, Eugene. *Tentacles Longer than Night: Horror of Philosophy*, Vol. 3. Washington: Zero Books, 2014.

Wang, David D. "Lu Xun, Han Song and the Unfinished Literary Revolution: 'Imagination' and 'Mentation'." [*Lu Xun, Han Song, yu wei wan de wenxue geming—'xuanxiang' yu 'shensi'*]. *Exploration and Free Views* [You xueshu de sixiang]. May, 2019: 48-51.

----. *The Monster that is History: History, Violence, and Fictional Writing in Twentieth-Century China*. Berkeley: University of California Press, 2004

Wang, Ping (王平). *A Cultural Study of Classical Chinese Fiction*. [Zhongguo gudai xiaoshuo wenhua yanjiu]. Jinan: Shandong Educational Press, 1996.

Wang Qin (王钦). "Frederic Jameson's 'Third World Literature' and 'National Allegory': A Defense." *Frontiers of Literary Studies in China*, 7.4 (Dec. 2013): 654-71.

Wang, Yao (王瑶). "Evolution or Samsara? Spatio-Temporal Myth in Han Song's Science Fiction." Tr. Nathaniel Isaacson. *Chinese Literature Today*, Vol. 7, #1 (2018): 23-27.

Zizek, Slavoj. *The Sublime Object of Ideology*. New York: Verso, 1989.

Zhang, Longxi. "Literary Modernity in Perspective." A Companion to Modern Chinese Literature, Ed. Zhang Yingjin. New York: Blackwell: 2016.

Acknowledgments

Research for this article was facilitated by a grant from the Ministry of Science and Technology of the Republic of China, Taiwan (2021-22).

Reviews

Wetmore Jr., Kevin J. *The Conjuring (Devil's Advocates)*. Liverpool: Auteur, 2021. 120 pp. ISBN 978-1-80034-397-9. $29.95.

The *Devil's Advocates* series of books has quickly become a new favorite among horror scholars. While each book takes an analytical look at a particular horror film, the approaches are wide ranging in both style and method. With an already extensive library of titles, this series provides a great entry point into horror scholarship. Kevin J. Wetmore Jr.'s *The Conjuring* is no exception. Author of *Post-9/11 Horror in American Cinema* and, most recently, *Eaters of the Dead: Myths and Realities of Cannibal Monsters*, Wetmore Jr. is a decorated scholar interested in a plethora of subjects besides horror and popular culture. Other interests include Asian cinema, African theater, and Shakespeare. In his *Devil's Advocates* entry, Wetmore Jr. primarily explores four main aspects of James Wan's *The Conjuring*. Chapter 1 focuses on *The Conjuring*'s perplexing R-rating and the film's "scary" factor. Chapter 2 switches its focus to the blurry lines between the real and cinematic portrayal of the film's main protagonists, the demonologists Ed and Lorraine Warren. Chapter 3 deals with the reoccurring motifs of children, their toys, and women (in both monstrous and human form), while the final chapter situates *The Conjuring* within its cinematic universe filled with sequels and spin-offs. As a whole, Wetmore Jr.'s *The Conjuring* is an insightful and well-researched book that fits nicely into *The Conjuring* cinematic universe's small but growing scholarship.

Written in an informal style, Wetmore Jr. brilliantly begins with a true story of his own—the time he got to visit the Warrens and the now infamous Annabelle doll (Wetmore Jr. 7-8). Not only is this a fun opening, but it reminds the reader that, while *The Conjuring* might be a horror film, it deals with real people, real events, and for some, real experiences. As Wetmore Jr. argues, *The Conjuring* is "culturally referential" (10) as it draws from paranormal investigative TV shows and other haunted house or possession films. What is important to note is that he also acknowledges that the film may be more resonant for Christian (especially Catholic) viewers. In addition, Wetmore Jr. states that *The Conjuring* works best if the viewer is knowledgeable of the horror genre since director James Wan's craftsmanship borrows from both contemporary and 70s horror (10). While the book offers plenty of informative analyses, Wetmore Jr.'s *The Conjuring* is also geared toward the broader fandom.

In "Chapter One: '"It's Right Behind You!' Or Rated-R for 'Terror,'" the author contemplates the film's odd R-rating. While *The Conjuring* has little gore or violence (no person dies in the film!), Wetmore Jr. argues that the "terror" comes from that which the viewer cannot see (15). The juxtaposition created by the onscreen characters' horrified gaze at an entity the viewer is unable to perceive creates a sense of dread. However, as Wetmore Jr. points out, these scenes are meticulously and expertly crafted by Wan. They unfold like "magic tricks," building one layer at a time. "The secret of *The Conjuring*," Wetmore Jr.

concludes, "is that the magic trick never stops – it continues throughout the film" (37). This chapter, while a good introduction of the film's style and background, is ultimately lighter on theoretical work than the chapters to come.

Horror scholars may find chapters two and three the most fruitful. Chapter Two, "The Warren Files Or 'Based On A True Story,'" explores the film's "different cultural realities" associated with the controversial demonologists (39). Wetmore Jr. investigates three in particular– the figures of Ed and Lorraine Warren as real people versus cinematic characters, the film's use of the ghost hunting TV aesthetic, and the portrayal of Catholicism (40). Wetmore Jr. successfully navigates horror scholarship's diverse fields, while drawing upon his own expertise in the field. He does particularly compelling work on linking *The Conjuring* to the larger cultural context of television ghost hunting series post-9/11. The blurry lines between the religious reality of the Warrens as Catholics, the reality of their cases/criticisms/skeptics, and the fictionalized Hollywood portrayal of their lives are a complex web to untangle, but Wetmore Jr. does so carefully and respectfully, making a strong case that these three aspects make the film feel "rooted in historic reality" despite many elements being fictitious (63).

Chapter Three, "Child's Play and Women's Work" then examines the depictions of women and children in the film, as well as the recurring motif of children's toys. Wetmore Jr. highlights the juxtaposition between child's play (both toys and games) and suspense, arguing that children's toys and their common games, such as Hide and Clap, become vehicles for the demonic threat. These toys provide the mediation between the supernatural and mundane world, allowing Wetmore Jr. to conclude "that the things we do and play in our youth is what haunts us in the future" (74). In addition, he also offers an intriguing discussion of the role of women in *The Conjuring*, highlighting that, while the film is female-centric, it is not necessarily feminist. In fact, Wetmore Jr. concludes the opposite: the film is conservative in terms of its representations of gender roles and conforms to established patriarchal expectations (76). The chapter provides a detailed consideration of gender and makes a convincing argument that the film's demonic presence is primarily rooted in traditional femininity.

The last chapter, "'Everything You See In Here Is Either Haunted, Cursed, Or Has Been Used In Some Kind Of Ritual Practice.' Or, The Endless *Conjuring* Universe," while important in situating *The Conjuring* in its broader cinematic universe, feels a bit less developed that the preceding ones. The first section serves as a sort of long form summary of the book's findings, while generalizing them to *The Conjuring*'s cinematic universe. While I do not take issue with the assertions that *The Conjuring* universe is a "supernatural," "female-centric," and "Roman Catholic" one, these individual claims deserve a more thorough analysis within the film's sequels and spin-offs. Notably, the summaries of each sequel and spin-offs (and of Wan's other works) that follow could have tied in more significantly to the book's main film.

Despite this, Wetmore Jr.'s entry to the *Devil's Advocates* series, is a well-researched, well-written, and all-around fun text for both fans of horror and horror scholars, with the second and third chapters likely being of most use to academics. Since *The Conjuring* has solidified itself as a significant horror text in recent years, this book could usefully be included as part of undergraduate film and/or popular culture studies courses that focuses on contemporary horror. Its lucid writing style, devoid of academic jargon, makes it approachable to fans of the horror genre, *The Conjuring* universe, and its director James Wan more broadly. *The Conjuring* is a versatile book that I can see having value in many contexts.

ZACHARY DOIRON is a PhD student at the University of Waterloo. His research focuses on the intersection between American evangelical culture and horror cinema.

153•Reviews

Pugh, Tison. *Harry Potter and Beyond: On J.K. Rowling's Fantasies and Other Fictions*. University of South Carolina Press, 2020. 152 pp. Paperback. ISBN: 978-1-64336-087-4. $19.99.

In his latest monograph, Tison Pugh, who has previously published several articles and monographs on queerness in the *Harry Potter* series, now focuses on the whole of Rowling's oeuvre. Pugh has structured his *Harry Potter and Beyond* according to different genres, using a thematic approach that scrutinizes intertextual and genre conventions in a combined perspective. Covering not only the seven *Harry Potter* novels but *The Casual Vacancy* and Rowling's most recent series, the *Cormoran Strike* mysteries written under the pseudonym Robert Galbraith, Pugh provides a broad but not in-depth overview of intertextual references and genre influences, and summarizes debates surrounding questions of literariness as well as the fictional universe's canon and its limits. Overall, his clear structure allows for many interesting connections and observations regarding Rowling's entire oeuvre.

In his introduction, Pugh reminds the readers of Rowling's contributions to charitable organizations and equity efforts; although he occasionally mentions gender identity, he generally skirts the heated debates surrounding Rowling's inflammatory tweets on the subject, the last of which took place after publication. Throughout *Harry Potter and Beyond*, Pugh uses interviews and other public statements by Rowling in which she either adds information to her fictional worlds or reflects on her work. Pugh adduces these quotes as a sometimes-authoritative secondary source and examines them in light of their correspondence with her fictional texts. However, his text does not always critically engage with questions concerning the authority of an author over her text. For example, can Rowling's statement about not setting out to write children's literature indeed be regarded as a valuable piece of information that changes the scholarly conception of her novels? (13). Pugh does not enter this debate, and problematically, the implied answers to such questions differ depending on the chapter. Some theoretical groundwork and Pugh's scholarly opinion would have added to the book's depth.

The first chapter, "The Fantasy Foundations of the Harry Potter Novels," deals with fantasy fiction, a genre referenced throughout all subsequent chapters. The second chapter, "Hogwarts and the School Story Tradition," explores themes of social class and multicultural environments under the umbrella of the British school story; for example, Pugh discusses the social contrast between the Malfoys and the Weasleys as well as Harry's position within the British class system. In the third chapter, "Harry Potter's Adolescence and the *Bildungsroman* Tradition," the focus is predominantly on Harry's moral and ethical development as well as on the series' moral and ethical development in general. Pugh argues that the Harry Potter novels are didactic, stimulating readers to think about these issues and causing the readers to reflect on how they would react in certain situations. The usage of the term *Bildungsroman* in this context will surprise many German scholars as the monograph's use of the term in relation to the "British bildungsroman tradition" (50), as well as its reference to the *Künstlerroman* (in the endnotes), is more capacious than the German definition.

In chapter four, "The Mysteries of Hogwarts," Pugh delivers a closer analysis of the series by way of mystery genre characteristics, explaining how the novels also have innovative properties and can be considered more than typical representatives of the genre. Dissimilar to traditional mystery stories, the novels contain, for example, Harry's romantic life as well as ambiguities and hidden meanings. Pugh concludes that these additional elements heighten the novels' re-readability, which is not a typical feature of the genre, as once the mystery is known, interest in re-reading the story is lost. At times, if readers of Pugh's text insist on an extremely deft handling of literary tropes, they might be disappointed, as when the author regards some genre characteristics of detective stories, such as interviewing witnesses, not as hallmarks of detective fiction but as bothersome cliches. In "Rowling's Allegories of Good and Evil," the last chapter dealing with specific Harry Potter novels, Pugh chiefly investigates allegorical aspects of the texts, in particular World War II and Christian references. He concludes in his analysis—in a manner similar to that of Albus Dumbledore—that Voldemort and Harry are different because of their moral choices. Thematically, this chapter ties together many significant threads, including the ongoing discussion of morality.

Chapter six, "The Evolving Harry Potter Canon," still centers on the narrative world of Harry Potter but looks beyond the main series, as Pugh discusses what could be considered canon in the context of the ever-evolving, cross-media approach by the author and many other contributors, both official and non-official. Pugh proposes that each reader construct their own individual canon—a fair conclusion, but one he could have tied to the questions of morality raised in earlier chapters. Additionally, Pugh could have examined the position and authority of Rowling as an author and linked it back to his introduction. These omissions lessen the impact of the work.

In his final chapter, "Out of the Wizarding World: *The Casual Vacancy* and the Robert Galbraith Murder Mysteries," Pugh addresses those novels of Rowling set outside the broader Harry Potter canon and revisits questions of genre and intertextuality. Regrettably, he again does so without furthering his previous discussions of morality and ethics. Significantly, the theme of class and the balancing of realistic versus fantastical narrative elements reappear proving themselves constant threads in Rowling's writing. In general, Pugh applauds the balance and mixture of genre and literary fiction in Rowling's work, and concludes that Rowling's use of intertextual references allows her both originality and connectivity.

As a whole, the monograph does not possess a stringent, overarching thesis and remains more of an overview. On the one hand, it summarizes each primary work, and on the other, it observes various details concerning the broader topics of genre and intertextuality. Pugh's text can be easily used as a beginner's guide to Rowling's works, but it does not include many new findings and therefore might not be as interesting for the advanced reader. For example, while Pugh addresses intertextuality with medieval literature, such as pointing out that the names of three Weasley characters draw upon Arthurian legend, he never goes into depth about such connections. Overall, the monograph does not overwhelm the reader with sources, even though at least one is provided for each theme or topic broached, but Pugh's lively writing style displays his love for the subject.

ANNA LÜSCHER, who holds an MA in English Literature from the University of Newcastle, England, and a second MA in German Literature from the University of Konstanz, is a doctoral researcher at the University of Konstanz, Germany. Her dissertation focuses on differences in liminality among E.T.A. Hoffmann's *Nachtstücke*, Conan Doyle's *Sherlock Holmes* stories, and J.K. Rowling's *Harry Potter* series. Her teaching centers on English and German romanticism as well as spatial theory and narratology in popular and fantastic literature.

Williams, Christy. *Mapping Fairy-Tale Space: Pastiche and Metafiction in Borderless Tales*. Detroit: Wayne State University Press, 2021. 221 pp. Paperback. ISBN 978-0814343838. $32.99.

Christy Williams approaches twenty-first-century fairy tales in *Mapping Fairy-Tale Space: Pastiche and Metafiction in Borderless Tales* by expanding on previous scholarship by Marina Warner and Christina Bacchilega, as well as Karen E. Row, that looked into the interconnected web that has become fairy tale and folk stories and their adaptations. Williams' research builds on this concept of the interconnected web by examining the metaphor of mapping found within a variety of contemporary fairy tale variants.

The study begins with an introduction providing a theoretical framework for the main terms she's employing—primarily fairy-tale pastiche and the mapping metaphor from which the monograph gets its title. After the introduction, the book is divided into two main parts that focus on the two different types of mapping that Williams employs: "[the first type] by combining individual tales into a single storyworld or [the second] by self-referentially turning to fairy tales for guidance" (2). Part I, "Mapping Fairy Tales," considers how the texts chosen literally remap well-known fairy tale stories into new spaces often creating new types of fairy tale worlds. As she says, "The shared storyworld reflects a reconfiguration of how we think about genre and individual stories as part of a larger landscape and as interconnected. The geographic metaphor of landscapes and maps is a figurative representation of the epistemological shift born of an increasingly interconnected world" (21). The variants in this section are probably more familiar to scholars and non-researchers who have watched or read twenty-first-century fairy tale stories such as ABC/Disney's *Once Upon a Time* and Marissa Meyers's *The Lunar Chronicles*. Lesser known to some would be Seanan McGuire's *Indexing* series, even though it has been analyzed by other scholars in the field. Part II, "Fairy Tale Maps," examines texts that use fairy tales as maps or guides to resolve the conflicts within the narratives, including *Secret Garden* (a Korean television drama) and three fictional short stories by Kelly Link. While the texts in this section may not be as well-known as those in Part I, particularly the Korean drama to Western audiences, Williams provides compelling critical analysis of these texts and clearly shows how fairy tales, stories that throughout time have been used as guidebooks for young women and children, continue to provide figurative and literal maps for how one should live their life as seen in the new versions of the stories.

The Introduction, "Remapping a Genre: Fairy-Tale Pastiche as Critical Mode," is important reading for scholars who may not be familiar with the foundational theories underlying Williams' argument. She sets up the connections among earlier scholarship by scholars such as Christina Bacchilega, Jack Zipes, and Vanessa Joosen, among many others. She also employs the concept of "fairy-tale pastiche," coined by Jeanna Jorgensen in her 2007 article, "A Wave of the Magic Wand: Fairy Godmothers in Contemporary American Media," which connects her argument to the postmodern concepts of pastiche and intertextuality, thereby allowing her to connect "fairy-tale pastiche" to her own analytical map that she draws around her texts.

Chapter 1, "Genre and Geography: ABC's *Once Upon a Time* and the Mapping of a Fairy-Tale Land," examines the extremely complex narrative of the 2011-2018 television show *Once Upon a Time*. Williams investigates how the main narrative of the show, where fairy tale characters have been magically forced to live in non-magical Storybrooke, Maine for the last twenty-eight years and are unable to return to their homes in the magical Enchanted Forest, provides an example of how fairy tale characters and their stories can coexist within the same storyworld (or multiple storyworlds as occurs throughout the seven seasons). Williams uses this interweaving of stories as an example of her remapping metaphor to show that the creation of new storyworlds, in this case both Storybrooke and the Enchanted Forest, establishes a new type of map for fairy tales where they can coexist in the same space.

In Chapter 2, "Genres Overlaid: Serialization and Hybridity in Marissa Meyer's *The Lunar Chronicles* and Seanan McGuire's *Indexing*," the blending of the science fiction genre in *The Lunar Chronicles* combines with "the familiar frame of the fairy tale [which] allows readers to focus on the inventive science-fiction aspects of the novel— such as dangerous Others, devastating plagues, and the politics of invasion— instead of the structure" (69). This is also shown to be the case with the procedural cop narrative in McGuire's *Indexing* where the genre expectations for both a detective story and the procedural cop narrative help the reader to focus on the critical commentary provided by the fairy tale narratives that are highlighted by the other genres present in the story.

Starting the next section, which focuses on fairy tale stories as guides/maps within a narrative, Chapter 3, "Asking for Directions: Metafiction and Metaphor in the Korean Drama *Secret Garden*," examines the melodramatic romance of Gil Ra-im and Kim Joo-won and the use of "The Little Mermaid" as a map for their relationship. Joo-won, a high-end department store CEO, and Ra-im, a famous stuntwoman, meet, but in contrast to expectations based on "Cinderella," do not immediately fall in love. Instead, Joo-won consciously rewrites "The Little Mermaid" as the framework for their romance, which Williams deftly analyzes by examining why this story doesn't work for the characters' romance. Williams also emphasizes how the class differences between the two characters are further heightened by Joo-won's insistence that their romance would be fleeting, and at the end, Ra-im would drift away from him like seafoam, further reinforcing his perception that her life is worth nothing to him. Ra-im's refusal to accept this type of romance where she has no value forces Joo-won to face the imperfections of his version, and he must rewrite it until he finds a version that fits their love story.

In Chapter 4, "Following Footsteps: Redrafting Fairy-Tale Maps in Kelly Link's Short Fiction," Williams traces the motifs of shoes and feet through three of Link's short stories: "Travels with the Snow Queen," "Shoe and Marriage," and "The Girl Detective." While using the motif of shoes might immediately conjure up the image of "Cinderella," only "Shoe and Marriage" uses that frame narrative as a source tale. "The Snow Queen" is the obvious source tale for the first story, and Williams focuses her critical analysis on how the character of Gerda walks on glass to find her hero: instead of this being a happily-ever-after romance, Gerda realizes that fairy tales are not good maps for one's life and that the old maps no longer work for modern women – a very postmodern feminist retelling. The other two stories show further examples of how fairy tales, as originally written down by Charles Perrault, the Brothers Grimm, and Hans Christian Andersen, no longer serve the same purposes as they once did, especially for young women, so women need to redraw their maps to fit the guidance that they need in the twenty-first century.

Williams' concluding chapter, "Collapsing Borders in the Age of the Internet," makes an interesting connection between the fairy tale stories she examined and how the lack of borders in online spaces have created a new avenue of connection for everyone. She also acknowledges that her research was limited and that there is a lot of space for further exploration into the topic of how twenty-first-century fairy tale variants use mapping as a figurative or literal concept within their framework. I could see further analysis of this motif in texts like Chris Colfer's *The Land of Stories* series where the two protagonists fall into a fairy-tale portal world through the fairy tale storybook and become part of the story as they have to navigate the map of the fairy tale land. I appreciate the acknowledgement that there is more work to do in this area because there are many other twenty-first-century fairy tales that exist in the same storyworld, which Williams briefly mentions in Chapter 2, but some of those stories combine stories into fairy tale pastiche for reasons that were not covered in Williams' study.

Overall, the concept of a map when analyzing fairy tales is interesting because many source fairy tales tend to exist in a land that is "far, far away" and "Once Upon a Time." The nebulousness of these settings and general nature of the stories allow them to be applied to any place and time, so the stories can speak to the cultural anxieties of different eras in order to be rewritten to fit the needs of different times and places. However, Williams' argument does work for twenty-first-century narratives because these stories do provide specific places that audiences can recognize. Her critical analysis of the written texts by Meyer, McGuire, and Link is complex without being verbose and can therefore serve students as well as professional researchers. My only critique of Williams' argument is that the analysis of the chapter on *Once Upon a Time* is not as in-depth as the other chapters, which could be easily explained by the complexity of the interwoven narratives within that storyverse. There is more plot summary in that chapter than in the others, and I was left wondering why the metaphoric map in this storyworld was so important. Overall, Williams' book successfully uses the concept of mapping to explore how twenty-first-century fairy tale narratives function.

ALEXANDRA LYKISSAS is a tenure-track Professor of Humanities at Seminole State College of Florida, where she teaches courses on 20th/21st century humanities; Women, Gender, and Culture; and contemporary popular culture. Her research focuses on how fairy-tale pastiche leads to character collaboration in order for characters to develop a resistance movement against the villain in the stories, which reflects twenty-first-century anxieties about authoritarianism. She is the author of "Popular Culture's Enduring Influence on Childhood: Fairy Tale Collaboration in the Young Adult Series *The Lunar Chronicles*" and "Cyborg-erella: Marissa Meyer's Cinder as a New Type of Other."

164•Reviews

Moody, Kyle A. and Nicholas A. Yanes, eds. Hannibal *for Dinner: Essays on America's Favorite Cannibal on Television*. Jefferson, NC: McFarland, 2021. 335 pgs. Paperback. ISBN: 978-1-4766-6642-6. $45.00.

Moody and Yanes's collection of essays explores the dignified cannibal of modern lore in his most recent iteration, the NBC series *Hannibal*. By cherry-picking areas of focus within the complicated, often multi-layered structure of the show, which showrunner Bryan Fuller is quoted here as calling "a pretentious art film from the 80s" (307), the text's editors, Kyle A. Moody and Nicholas A. Yanes, have both contributed to and assembled a crack team of *Hannibal* investigators, whose talents include and move beyond academia. Considering the television series' content, it seems only right to include in the collection, among others, the perspectives of artists, writers, and a pastry chef. The collection's larger work is to dissect specific intersecting elements in the television universe (crafted largely through Fuller's vision) of Hannibal Lecter and his friends, enemies, and victims—in Lecter's world, there is often a Venn diagram betwixt these categorizations. The character's duality as a cannibalistic serial killer and a genteel practicing psychiatrist has long fascinated consumers of both Thomas Harris's work in the books that originated the good doctor, as well as the films that adapt and depict Lecter's clever criminal mischief.

The collection concentrates, in surprisingly large part, on peeking behind the curtain to see how such sumptuous sausage is made: Interviews with producers and writers on the show are peppered in every few chapters, working to break up the essay format of the text and pull the reader out of abstract musings on aesthetics and the blurred boundaries of self and others to step back and consider the work that went into creating that effect. Additionally, multiple essays address the dynamic relationship between the show's creators and fans that sets *Hannibal* apart from other shows. The collection relies on the overlap between its essay themes, which at times can be, perhaps, a bit too much overlap—there are some repetitive discussions of Fuller's status as a fan of the *Hannibal* world, the show's driving force, and audience mediator, for example—but most of the essays offer original and insightful perspectives that anyone who has interest in the show, the world of Harris's stories, and/or the many ways in which themes of fandom, aesthetics, food, bodies, and deliberately blurred boundaries can be skillfully dissected, should consume with no small degree of delight.

    A particular strength of the collection is its attention to detail; the Introduction, clearly paying playful tribute to the meal-associated episode titles, is subtitled "The Hors d'Oeuvres," and Moody and Yanes start off by explaining the unique ingredients of the collection (in all things Hannibal Lecter, the pun is intended) and their inspiration for creating the work. "Hannibal was art that inspired devotion and interest," they explain, and it is that devotion and interest that is at the heart of both the art and its scholarship (2). Kirsty Worrow's "My Darling Cannibal: The Mechanics of Perverse Allegiance in Hannibal" distinguishes usefully between the fans' anticipated alignment with Will Graham and their aforementioned perverse allegiance toward Hannibal. It touches on an interesting conundrum for fans: how to reconcile the elements of Hannibal Lecter they are drawn to with his horrific crimes? Worrow also notes how Hannibal is recontextualized and understood as a character by fans: the appeal of the "cathartic pleasure" of eating the rude, the "defanging" woobification of the character, and transformative works (39-40). This is followed neatly by Nicole Michaud Wild's "Empathy for the Audience: *Hannibal*, the Fannibals and What Happens When A Show Takes Its Fandom Seriously," a piece that discusses the dynamic relationship between fans of the series, called "Fannibals," and the show's creators, most notably Fuller, and how this impacted the show. Wild also notes that the main character Will Graham's empathy "elevates emotion, stereotypically a vilified feminine quality, to the status of essentially the cure for violence" (53). In Megan Fowler's "'If I saw you every day, forever, I'd remember this time': Deconstructing Gender Performance and Heteronormativity Through Adaptation," the essay explores the show's reworking of the franchise as "supplanting of the original" with Will as Clarice Starling—sometimes even at the level of dialogue—and ponders both the loss of leading feminist figures in the text as well as the queered intertextuality of key romantic scenes, now between Will and Hannibal (114).

Each essay explores a different facet of *Hannibal*'s engagement with bodies. Lisa Rufus' "Giving Voice to the Unmentionable: How Hannibal Lecter Uses Bodies in the Television Series *Hannibal*" explores in part how the body, living or dead, can be used by Hannibal to communicate something. Even when his kills are an adaptation of another murderer's work, the forms they take signal Hannibal's skill and artistic prowess. Multiple essays remark on the aesthetic sensibility of the cannibal, and Rufus notes that Hannibal's "compulsion for artistic dominance" takes his interest in adapting the crimes of others and "adds his own signature, making them his own works" (10). Rufus's work also provides behind-the-curtain information for viewers: how a cannibal may be classified, who designs the deceptively tempting-looking food, and how sound and visuals work together to communicate to the audience. "Bodies That Change: Transformation, Body Dysmorphia and the Malleability of Identity in Bryan Fuller's Hannibal" by Samantha McLaren takes the body in a different direction; here, the body is physically a "site for transformation, and as a material that is susceptible to being transformed," and its boundaries are destabilized (72). What is particularly of interest here is McLaren's exploration of how the boundaries of the mind and body are collapsed by Hannibal. Physically, "Cannibalism is the most blatant act of border-crossing in the series, the moment at which the body of one becomes incorporated into the body of another," but this cannibalism can also cross over into the mind: "The cannibal's quest to get inside Graham's head involves a number of physical penetrations as well" (80, 85). Lorianne Reuser's "Go with the Flow: Will Graham and Liminality in Bryan Fuller's *Hannibal*" also explores the blurring of binaries, but here Reuser discusses the significance of liquid and fluidity as applied to Will Graham, the dream-plagued empath. She notes that "the liminal can be a site of empowerment through instability" and it is when Will is in a liminal state that he is able to see things clearly; like many other essays in the collection, Reuser plays well with language, describing "elements of Will's unconscious that overflow their containers" (129-130, 132).

The nightmare-like visions and scenes of carnage that Will grows accustomed to are interestingly linked to art, as well; as Vittoria Lion points out, "Often described with the metaphor of ruminating on oneself, dreaming and introspection can be viewed as cannibalistic" (145). In "Eating Exquisite Corpses and Drinking New Wine: The Chesapeake Ripper as the Authentic Surreal Murderer," Lion places Hannibal's murders in the tradition of "Paris-centered early twentieth century Surrealist groups," a reading that points out the strangeness of the fact that "in the universe of *Hannibal*, every murderer appears to be an artist" (139, 143). Although the essay is informative about Surrealism, and clever in locating its parallels in the series, Lion's work could easily also branch out into a related discussion of Hannibal's place within modern society as an unusually avant-garde artist, as she notes "Both Hannibal and Desnos' Ripper are invisible to those bound to the routines of industrial society" (150). In the same way, Megan McAllister's "Food Culture in *Hannibal*," although delivering delightfully on symbolic food, flowers, and décor in the show, could have been expanded further, perhaps put into a larger conversation with the "cooking show aesthetic" discussed earlier in the collection in Naja Later's "Cannibalizing *Hannibal*: The Horrific and Appetizing Rewriting of *Hannibal* Mythology" (93). In "It's a Matter of Taste: Bourdieu and the Impeccably Mannered Anthropophagite," Sarah Cleary uses sociologist Pierre Bourdieu's treatise on taste to talk about Hannibal's views towards humanity, and how humans can be transformed to food in his eyes: "Hannibal's taste for human flesh is not so much the defining attribute of his pathology but rather a symptom of his systematic classification of humanity as beneath him" (198). Cleary takes Bourdieu's assertion that "taste is essentially used to distinguish between the various social classes" and creates an impressive reading about

Lecter's table manners and cooking delicacies as "social weapons" (203). Several other essays hint temptingly at talking about class and society in *Hannibal*, but perhaps another volume exploring more of the manifold aspects of the text could expand on eating the rude versus eating the rich.

I would highly recommend this text for fans of the series and Hannibal Lecter universe; students of fandom, film and television studies may also find this work very useful for understanding a criminally underrated television series that nevertheless created an enthusiastic fan community through its depictions of intricate, intimate, and artistic brutality.

KATHLEEN SHAUGHNESSY is a PhD Candidate at the University of Iowa. Her research interests include medicine, crime, science, and the Gothic in nineteenth-century British literature.

170•Reviews

Rickels, Laurence, *Critique of Fantasy, Vol 1: Between a Crypt and a Datemark*. Punctum Books, 2020. 254 pp. Cloth. ISBN 978-1950192922. $22.00.

Rickels, Laurence, *Critique of Fantasy, Vol 2: The Contest Between B-Genres*. Punctum Books, 2020. 234 pp. Cloth. ISBN 978-1953035189. $22.00.

Rickels, Laurence, *Critique of Fantasy, Vol 3: The Block of Fame*. Punctum Books, 2021. 240 pp. Cloth. ISBN 978-1953035288. $22.00.

At the end of 1907, Freud delivered his paper, "Creative Writers and Day-Dreaming," which focuses on the role of fantasy in psychoanalysis. This was a time of great change for the doctor: the first signs of the international recognition of his work were appearing, yet he was still holding his training sessions for other psychoanalysts not in a clinic or school, but on walks around his neighborhood. At this moment of standing on the precipice of world-wide fame, in front of an audience of 90, in the rooms of Viennese publisher Hugo Heller, Freud described how fantasies rip childhood wishes out of the past and turn them into dreams of the future.

In his talk, Freud is first interested in how writers get their ideas. He suggests looking for the roots of adult creativity in the play of children, since "we can never give anything up; we only exchange one thing for another" (Freud "Creative Writers," 145). In adulthood, play is exchanged for fantasizing and daydreaming, and it is in the daydream that a particular temporality becomes apparent.

171•Reviews

Daydreams are not removed from reality. They are not unalterable archetypes floating around in the unconscious. Rather, daydreams are time-bound, reflecting changes in the daydreamer's life. Thus, daydreams bear a "date-mark" (*Zeitmarke*) ("Creative Writers," 147) which stamps them with whatever happens to be important at the time the fantasy is fantasized. This opens up a discussion of the temporality of daydreams, which, like Freud's endopsychic structure of the id, ego, and superego, is threefold: first, the present daydream is triggered by some current impression; then, this reaches back to a previous event in which a similar wish was fulfilled in the past (such as in childhood); and, finally, the daydreamer now images a future situation in which this same childhood wish is once again fulfilled.

Freud gives a rather straight-forward example to illustrate this daydream temporality. An orphan boy, on his way to a job interview, daydreams that he will not only be successful in his job but will eventually marry the boss's daughter and take over the business. With this daydream, the boy has regained what he supposedly only had as a young child: a happy home and protective parents. "Thus past, present and future are strung together, as it were, on the thread of the wish that runs through them," Freud says ("Creative Writers," 148), meaning that a fulfilled wish in the past becomes the hopeful fulfillment of a daydream in the future.

Laurence Rickels's three-volume work, *Critique of Fantasy*, is centered on how the temporality of the daydream becomes a method to incorporate mourning into our lives. As former professor of comparative literature and German at the University of California at Santa Barbara, Rickels uses a wide variety of examples from literature, film, and art to explore and expand this new daydream function.

The first volume is subtitled *Between a Crypt and a Datemark*. Both terms relate to Freud's temporality, but with a twist. For Freud, daydreams involve the past because they project an old fulfilled wish out into the future. But the crypt is a different animal. Initially developed by psychoanalysts Nicolas Abraham and Mária Török, the crypt is not a sanctuary for pleasant wishes fulfilled, but rather a vault for losses that are too traumatic to confront fully. Thus, when the daydreamer reaches back and pulls something out of the crypt to insert into their daydream, a different set of coordinates arises. Rather than being about wish-fulfillment, the daydream is now retooled into a process for confronting traumatic loss or, in other words, into a process for mourning. Thus, with the crypt, as Rickels puts it, the temporality of the daydream gets turned into "the two times you get and the one time you forget" (vol. 1, 57).

To get a taste of Rickels's methodology, we can see an example of this process in the movie *Jurassic World* (2015), the fourth installment of the *Jurassic Park* franchise. In the earlier films, attempts to create a theme park featuring genetically engineered dinosaurs are thwarted by the animals escaping their confines and causing havoc. Yet in the 2015 movie, which is set 22 years after the original, a fully functioning dino-theme park is in place, and the issues that plagued the first films have seemingly been overcome.

Well, at least until the crypt gets involved. In one scene, two brothers enter an out-of-bounds area and discover the ruins of the original park. They use the debris they find there to construct a Jeep and return to the main resort. For

Rickels, this scene is not one of wish-fulfillment in the sense that the 2015 park fulfills the wishes that business tycoon John Hammond had for opening a park in the original films. Instead, the scene functions as a crypt in that it is a storehouse for the trauma, death, and loss from the first films that have never been properly dealt with, hence the new park and its new havoc: "The secret raptor provenance is the hot spot of betrayal and allegiance in the heroic saga waged among the creatures" (vol. 1, 25).

Although *Jurassic World* is usually considered a work of science fiction, this scene of the crypt is read as a moment where fantasy creeps in. Here Rickels joins a long line of thought that does not see the genres of sf and fantasy diametrically opposed to each other, although the conclusions he makes from their border crossings is unique: they become a strategy for mourning.

For policing the borders of fantasy, Rickels turns to J.R.R. Tolkien's essay, "On Fairy-Stories," composed during the writing of *Lord of the Rings* (1954–55). Although Tolkien spends most of his essay arguing for what a work of fantasy is not, including banning the use of any kind of dreaming, he does eventually define the genre as covering great swathes of space and time and featuring relations with non-human beings. Yet in the midst of this border patrol, what interests Rickels most is how science fiction slips back into the discussion. Tolkien argues that the Eloi and Morlocks of H.G. Wells' *The Time Machine* (1895) exist in an "'abyss of time so deep as to work an enchantment upon them'" (qtd. in vol. 1, 38), meaning that even though time travel takes place through the technology of science fiction, these creatures are figures of fantasy because they are non-dreamed and reach back far into time.

Following this logic, in science fiction film, fantasy can also make an appearance, although Rickels argues that this happens in a rather peculiar moment: in the special effects that nearly define the genre. Special effects are read as the daydreams of science fiction, as the escape hatch for what we do not understand: "*Critique of Fantasy* follows the rebound of wish fantasy between literary description of the ununderstood and its cinematic counterpart (for example, visual and special effects)" (vol. 1, 22). With special effects, science fiction "can go into reverse and sustain within its ruins the allegorical legibility of deregulated fantasy" (vol. 1, 30). This crossing of the streams of fantasy and science fiction then opens "a forum for addressing novel forms of grief" (vol. 1, 33) because one genre functions as the crypt for the unresolved loss of the other.

In order better to understand how such crypts function, we should turn to the second volume of Rickels' trilogy, where a number of rather unexpected works are corralled into the science fiction/fantasy mix. *The Mystery of Picasso* is Henri-Georges Clouzot's 1956 documentary in which the artist creates his work on glass plates so that the camera can go "behind" the canvas to show the man at work. What makes this film science-fictional is Picasso's encounter with the technology of the production, including the whole set-up of the camera and glass plate, Clouzot counting down the remaining feet of film stock and pressuring Picasso to finish his painting in time, and the director at one point running the film in reverse "to redo or undo the painting process we just witnessed" (vol. 2, 49). These inclusions of special effects within the film function as sites of fantasy, where unconscious wish fulfillment can take place:

Pablo Picasso made no bones about the wish that he brought to his encounters with technical media, first photography, then film. It was to see conserved the successive changes going into a work, which are lost upon completion of the process. The mediatic prospect of simultaneity of visualization or remembrance was the place Freud marked in his book of analogues for unconscious thought. (vol. 2, 47)

Yet the technology in the Picasso film has a slightly different function than how fantasy has been developed so far. Rather than acting merely as a crypt, these "special effects" also take on the role of Freud's mystic writing pad, since "Each station of the film is demarcated in the manner of the mystic writing pad lifting away one image from the screen to clear it for the next image in progress" (vol. 2, 49). Freud's 1925 "A Note on the Mystic Writing-Pad" is based on a re-usable writing device, a wax slab covered with transparent sheets so that one can write something and then lift the sheet and the writing supposedly "disappears." However, the device is imperfect and traces of writing remain, prompting Freud to take it as "a concrete representation of the way in which I tried to picture the functioning of the perceptual apparatus of our mind" (Freud "A Note," 232). The glass plate in the Picasso film has a similar role. The artist works and re-works his pictures over and over, for example staring with a rooster and then ending up with a human face, although with a rooster partially visible underneath. This represents a different approach to fantasy since it focuses on fantasy's simultaneity, overlap, and doubledness, as seen in the multiple versions of a drawing all appearing together at once.

The example of Picasso appears in the second volume of Rickels's trilogy, subtitled *The Contest between B-Genres*, and in fact most of its examples come from the world of B-movies and books, including *Tarzan the Ape Man* (1932), C.S. Lewis' *Space Trilogy* (1938-1945), *Zardoz* (1974), and, rather impressively, *Batteries Not Included* (1987). The strata of the writing pad act as a key interpretive tool for these examples, as does another multi-layered psychoanalytic concept, the transitional object.

English psychoanalyst D. W. Winnicott's idea of the transitional object was first published in 1951. Transitional objects are a part of child development and are situated between a child's instinctual play, say with their own fists and fingers (by putting them into their mouths), and their play with objects which are seen as separate from themselves, as "not-me" objects, such as dolls. As Winnicott says, transitional objects, lying between these two, have some of the properties of both:

> By this definition an infant's babbling and the way in which an older child goes over a repertory of songs and tunes while preparing for sleep come within the intermediate area as transitional phenomena, along with the use made of objects that are not part of the infant's body yet are not fully recognized as belonging to external reality. (Winnicott 266-67)

Here we can see how transitional objects relate to the writing pad and the daydream: all involve overlap, or a not letting go, which Rickels then repurposes into a site for confronting loss.

At first glance, Edgar Rice Burroughs's novel *Tarzan of the Apes* (1912) seems to feature a key transitional site in the form of the small cabin in the "primeval" forest which held the bones of Tarzan's parents, whose death lead to Tarzan being raised by some local "apes" and whose lock Tarzan struggles to open, never having learned to differentiate between a wall and a door. Yet Rickels reads the novel differently, stating that, "Although the cabin of Tarzan's birth houses the skeletons of his dead parents (and of his ape mother's dead baby), it isn't a crypt but a storehouse of knowledge, a school library and class-room. It's where Tarzan, beginning in adolescence, comes into his inheritance. The cabin of reason supplies his epistemophilia" (vol. 2, 27).

Instead, the kind of overlapping Winnicott describes is turned into both a theme of work examined and an actual interpretive tool in Rickels's third volume, *The Block of Fame*. One of the prime examples therein is Susan Sontag's teenage visit to Thomas Mann in Los Angeles in 1949. Just sixteen at the time (although she had graduated from high school a year earlier), Sontag had thought *The Magic Mountain* one of the great works of art, yet when she finally met the author she was filled with shame at Mann's facileness. While this example might be taken as Sontag daydreaming about what Mann would be like based on a wish he had had when she was younger, Rickels does not stop there: he intersperses his reading of the interview with a totally different text, an analysis of the way the Gidget novels and films upend their expected beach-blanket banality with references to the likes of Marcus Aurelius, Keats, Shelley, and Vittorio de Sica. These two examples are mixed together to such a degree that we end up with passages such as the following, which represents the multilayers of the writing pad, or the transitional object that will not let one side let go of the other:

178•Reviews

The Sontag who graduated from North Hollywood High School at age fifteen might be characterized, like the subtitle to *Gidget*, as the little girl with big ideas. Little, however, in the sense of young: Sontag was the tallest girl in her class. Just as Kathy Kohner a.k.a. Franzie Hofer a.k.a. Gidget was mediated as somewhat laughable, though charmingly so, through the midlife criticism of her father Frederick Kohner, who, as the author of the 1957 coming-of-age book, mimicked and ventriloquated her, so teen Susan, as recalled by Sontag from the other shore of fulfillment of the wish to be an important intellectual author, is a touch ridiculous for the purity of her aspiration to become the big-ideas version of herself. (vol. 3, 124)

Rickels then uses this technique of reading one-with-the-other to discuss Robert Wilson's portraits of Lady Gaga and Marina Abramović's planned film about James Franco, among many other unexpected couplings.

Yet all the examples are not so easy-going. Rickels explores how the accusations of sexual assault and misconduct against Brett Kavanaugh, Trump's 2018 Supreme Court nominee, would never have had any sway with those who had already voted for the "Grab 'em by the pussy" president, and thus functioned as a distraction for any other crimes the candidate may have committed. In another engaged example, the special effects of *2001: A Space Odyssey* (1968) are set against cinematographer and artist Arthur Jafa's reading of the film as a complete occlusion of any signs of blackness that is actually a *preoccupation* with blackness, as seen in the dark monolith at the film's center, a true site of mourning.

There is little more we can ask from theory than to see things differently, and this cross-pollination of an abundance of examples does just that. Fantasy becomes a mode of critique, meaning a mode of reading the world around us, to the point that everything everywhere seems to relate to it. It gets so bad that when you read the first lines of Andrea Lawlor's novel *Paul Takes the Form of a Mortal Girl* (2017), "Like a shark, Paul had to keep moving. He slept only when necessary" (Lawlor 3), it is hard not to see it as a description of the sleepy-yet-awake feeling of a daydream, and when Charlie Gere's first essay in *I Hate the Lake District* (2020) begins with "I decided to find a Japanese garden I had read about that still exists in the Eskdale Valley. The idea of such a garden in Cumbria seemed to me to be vastly incongruous, and, yet, in some way appropriate, though at the time of setting out I was not sure why" (Gere 25), you feel like you know why already, since the garden obviously functions as a colonialist fantasy, date-stamped with the moment of its creation, *incongruous* because it does not belong, *appropriate* because it represents the wish-fulfillment of England's colonialist past.

Through all of these examples, and more, Rickels's trilogy develops fantasy as a framework for understanding, meaning that it functions as a site for mourning what we did not know we just could not let go. He shows how our past is still waiting to happen.

Works Cited

Freud, Sigmund. "A Note Upon the 'Mystic Writing Pad.'" *The Standard Edition of the Complete Psychological Works of Sigmund Freud, Volume XIX (1923-1925)*. Edited by James

Strachey. Hogarth Press and the Institute of Psycho-Analysis, 1961: 226-232.

---. "Creative Writers and Day-Dreaming." *The Standard Edition of the Complete Psychological Works of Sigmund Freud, Volume IX (1906-1908)*. Edited by James Strachey. Hogarth Press and the Institute of Psycho-Analysis, 1959: 141-153.

Gere, Charlie. *I Hate the Lake District*. Goldsmiths Press, 2019.

Lawlor, Andrea. *Paul Takes the Form of a Mortal Girl*. Vintage, 2019.

Winnicott, D.W. *The Collected Works of D.W. Winnicott, Volume 9 1969-1971*. Oxford University Press, 2017.

BRIAN WILLEMS is associate professor of literature and film at the University of Split, Croatia. He is most recently the author of *Zugov učinak* (Multimedia institute Zagreb, 2022), *Sham Ruins: A User's Guide* (Routledge, 2021), and *Speculative Realism and Science Fiction* (Edinburgh University Press, 2017). He is also the author of the novella *Henry, Henry* (Zero Books, 2017) and has curated exhibitions of new media in Croatia and Slovenia.

www.ingramcontent.com/pod-product-compliance
Lightning Source LLC
Chambersburg PA
CBHW011758040426
42446CB00018B/3451